The HEALTHY BRAIN Cookbook

We all know that eating well is crucial to so many aspects of our health, but the benefits extend far beyond simply helping us stay in good shape. Research has shown how maintaining a balanced, nutritious diet is one of the best things you can do for long-term brain health, something we all need to look after as we age.

In this book, you can learn more about the everyday ingredients linked to improved brain function, and those that may even help protect us against cognitive decline and dementia. This cookbook features over 50 delicious recipes that are rich in the brain-supporting nutrients shown to improve your cognition and boost your mood.

CONTENTS

Eating for a healthy brain 006

SALADS & LIGHT BITES

Green goddess soup 016
Taco salad in tortilla 'bowls' 018
Chicken & avocado Caesar salad 020
Avocado, bacon, pecan
& chicory salad 022
Borlotti bean & kale soup 024
Herring smørrebrød 026
Mackerel superfood salad 028
Prawn & broccoli rice bowl 030
Crowd-pleaser kedgeree 032
Sardines with avocado salsa 034
Poke bowl 036
Veggie ramen 038
Gado gado 040
Broccoli, beet & grain salad 042
Wild rice salad with miso dressing 044

MEAT, POULTRY & VEG

Rosemary, cranberry, juniper
& beef casserole 048
Chicken stew with sauerkraut 050
Duck & healthy greens salad 052
Flaxseed houmous & spiced lamb 054
Miso pork with root vegetable chips ... 056
Walnut & sesame pesto
pasta with crispy sausage 058
Aromatic fried rice & eggs 060
Spicy Turkish eggs
with tahini yogurt 062
Edamame, cottage cheese
& new potato frittata 064
Super-greens veg & tofu stir-fry 066
Tofu skewers & noodle salad 068

FISH & SEAFOOD

Sicilian-style mackerel	072
Malaysian fish curry	074
Fishcakes with spicy dressing	076
Oat-&-sesame-crusted salmon with blistered tomatoes	078
Salmon & spaghetti bolognese	080
Salmon mac 'n' cheese with kimchi	082
Miso-glazed salmon & kimchi fried rice	084
Sardine & spinach panzanella	086
Roast trout stuffed with herb quinoa & peppers	088
Mustard & leek trout	090

SWEETS & DRINKS

Kefir fruit & bran bowl	094
Best blueberry crumble muffins	096
Nut, seed & berry crumble	098
Apple & blueberry flapjacks	100
Super berry breakfast bowl	102
Cranberry muesli bars	104
Dark chocolate mousse	106
Sugar plums	108
Super smoothies	110

EATING FOR A HEALTHY BRAIN

EATING FOR A HEALTHY BRAIN

Your nutritional choices can impact your current and future brain function; let's take a look at why this is and find out what you should be putting on your plate...

INTRO

We know that it's important to look after our physical health and our mental health, but what about our brain health? The brain is a complex and important organ that works for us on so many different levels. It helps us to understand and control day-to-day movement; it looks after all our cognitive, mental and emotional processes; and it affects the way we behave, including our understanding of social conventions. If your brain function is suboptimal or starts to decline, this can have a huge impact on your physical, mental and emotional wellbeing.

There are many factors that contribute to the health of the brain. Your activity levels can have a big impact; regular exercise has been shown in numerous studies to have a positive effect on brain health. Socialising and connecting with others also helps to stimulate and activate parts of the brain. Getting enough sleep helps the brain to function optimally and repair, while chronic stress can shrink the prefrontal cortex, which can reduce memory function.

WHY DOES DIET MAKE A DIFFERENCE?

One area that is emerging as incredibly important is the role that our diet plays in maintaining and improving brain health. What you eat impacts the way your body works, including heart function and blood vessel health – we know that a diet that's high in saturated fat, for example, can lead to higher blood pressure and blocked arteries. Your blood vessels are responsible for supplying essential nutrients and oxygen to your organs; as the brain is an organ, it makes sense that having a healthy body means a good flow of blood and nutrients to the brain, and hence better brain health. Not only that, what you eat can contribute to levels of inflammation in the brain, as well as how much energy it produces. Dietary factors can also affect how the brain's cells communicate, so optimum nutrition can help retain optimum communication.

"The right diet can boost your mental health and wellbeing, lowering your risk of depression"

The right diet can help support and protect your brain health in a number of different ways, it can:

- Improve your mental health and wellbeing, lowering your risk of depression and anxiety, as well as helping you to manage stress.
- Contribute to better focus, memory and overall cognitive ability.
- Boost your motivation and help you to control your emotions.
- Help you to be more physically active, and get better sleep.
- Protect your brain against age-related degradation, and reduce your risk of neurological diseases, such as Alzheimer's, Parkinson's and more.

Staying physically, mentally and socially active is beneficial for your brain

EATING FOR A HEALTHY BRAIN

All of these benefits will hugely and positively impact your daily life, making it incredibly important to prioritise your brain health.

Even making small changes to your current diet could have a big impact on your brain health – in both the short term and long term – as well as your longevity. What you eat can have both positive and negative effects; there are foods that will boost brain health and those that might be more detrimental. However, an all-or-nothing approach is often hard to maintain and can be overwhelming. So, focus on a few things you can start adding to your diet straight away to gain the immediate benefits, then you can look at longer-term changes to the way you eat over time.

WHAT IS A BRAIN-HEALTHY DIET?

A brain-healthy diet doesn't have to be complicated. One of the eating plans most frequently cited for optimal health is the Mediterranean diet. Researchers are currently conducting studies to try and figure out why this particular way of eating seems to be so good for us. It is associated with better outcomes across the board – better brain health, physical health and mental health; decreased chance of certain diseases and illnesses; and improved energy and focus. The Mediterranean diet is quite similar in structure to the NHS Eatwell Guide in the UK and the Healthy Eating Plate in the USA. It focuses on eating plenty of whole, unprocessed plant-based foods, such as wholegrains, legumes, lentils, nuts and seeds. It also includes fruits and vegetables, healthy fats (predominantly olive oil in Mediterranean cuisine), oily fish, and moderate portions of lean white meat.

Those who naturally eat a Mediterranean-style diet have better health outcomes, so scientists and researchers are keen to discover exactly why this is. One thing that is clear is that the foods that are good for the heart and cardiovascular health, are also good for brain health. What this also indicates is that the risk factors for cardiovascular disease are also risk factors for diseases like dementia. Alzheimer's Research UK undertook some research that involved looking at previous studies involving thousands of participants, where they provided information about their diet, as well as taking memory and cognitive tests. What was shown was that those who followed a more Mediterranean-style diet performed better on tests of brain function.

Published in 2023 in the journal *Frontiers in Public Health*, a review article titled 'Nutrition and cognitive health: A life course approach' brought together a body of evidence into the impact of following a brain-healthy diet. As well as the Mediterranean diet, it also found the Nordic diet, DASH (Dietary Approaches to Stop Hypertension) diet and MIND diet to be linked to a lower risk of cognitive decline and dementia.

Eating a balanced diet rich in nutritious whole foods will help keep your body and mind healthy

INTRO

> "The MIND diet is specifically tailored towards brain health"

THE MIND DIET

All this research has helped us to discover the key nutrients that contribute to optimum health, which we should all try and incorporate into our diets.

The MIND diet is specifically tailored towards brain health and prevention of later-life cognitive decline. It combines the learnings from both the Mediterranean and DASH diets – its name stands for Mediterranean-DASH Intervention for Neurodegenerative Delay – which promotes a healthy, balanced plate, high in plant-based foods and low in saturated fat. However, the MIND diet goes a step further by actively encouraging individual nutrients that are shown to help with brain function, leading to improved memory, increased focus and better mental health; as well as recommending foods that should be limited due to their negative impact on brain health.

It is built around a series of recommendations, guidelines and daily/weekly serving suggestions, though these vary slightly in different studies and reports. Meals should be built around wholegrains, like oats, brown rice, quinoa, bulgur or wild rice – ideally

EATING FOR A HEALTHY BRAIN

WHAT ABOUT GUT HEALTH?

Looking after your gut microbiome could also have a positive impact on your brain

Scientists are rapidly learning more and more about the role of the gut in our overall health and wellbeing. There is a recognised link between the gut and the brain, often called the 'gut-brain axis', which refers to the two-way communication that happens between the emotional and cognitive centres of the brain and the intestinal functions.

According to the team at Zoe (zoe.com), there is increasing evidence that improving the health of your gut microbiome can reduce symptoms of mental health conditions, such as anxiety and depression. An article in *Frontiers in Public Health* suggests that: "Immune cells, cytokines, and chemokines are the microbiome's mechanisms for interacting with the brain, regulating brain processes and vice versa. The gut microbiota may modulate brain function and development through such immune signalling, as well as endocrine and neural pathways."

It's emerging research, but the best diet for gut health is very similar to that which we've outlined here for brain health, so by following the principles, you could optimise both your gut and brain function, which will then work together to improve your overall wellbeing. You should also look at introducing fermented foods to your diet. These foods contain good bacteria that help to restore and retain a balanced gut microbiome. Now early research is showing that these fermented foods are good for healthy brain function too – they may help to produce serotonin, which helps to stabilise moods. Try sauerkraut, kefir, kombucha, kimchi or miso, for example.

three servings a day. Wholegrains are high in fibre, which helps to maintain the gut microbiome, another factor in brain health (see boxout, left), and they also contain magnesium, which may contribute to higher brain volume. Vegetables should be included daily, with a strong focus on green leafy vegetables, such as spinach, kale and chard. These are packed with antioxidants, including folate and beta carotene, as well as vitamin K, which has been linked with improved cognitive function. Every week you should include nuts, beans and berries as well, all considered to be brain-healthy foods. It is not a totally plant-based diet, and it allows for a couple of meals a week based on poultry and at least one meal including oily fish.

When it comes to limiting foods, the MIND diet suggests no more than five servings per week of foods such as pastries or sweets, less than four servings of red meat, less than one serving of cheese and fried foods, and no more than a tablespoon of butter per day.

Various studies of the MIND diet have found a favourable link between lower rates of Alzheimer's disease and high MIND diet scores. It has also been linked to better cognitive function, larger brain volume, better memory and increased focus. While clinical studies are ongoing to prove the effectiveness of the MIND diet, its principles, like those of the Mediterranean and DASH diets, do include a lot of nutrients that have been linked to better brain health (see our guide to the 'Top 10 brain-boosting nutrients' on the following pages) in studies, which is likely why they are so effective.

MAKING CHANGES TO YOUR DIET

The Global Council on Brain Health is an independent collaborative bringing together experts from all fields to debate the latest in brain health science. They have created a detailed report that gives recommendations on which foods should be limited or included in an adult's diet. These recommendations are quite straightforward and can be a good place to start if you want to begin making changes to your nutrition to support your brain health. They sensibly point out that "no single food acts as a silver bullet for improving or maintaining brain health", but a healthy, varied diet with a range of nutrients is best.

Their recommendations actively encourage berries (but not as juice), fresh vegetables (with a focus on leafy greens), healthy fats (including extra-virgin olive oil), nuts, and fish and seafood – choosing whole, unprocessed foods where possible. They also suggest including beans and other legumes, fruits, low-fat dairy, poultry and grains. Fried foods, pastries, processed foods (especially processed meats), red meat, whole-fat dairy and salt should be limited, and trans fats avoided. They also encourage moderating alcohol if you drink it (and not to start drinking it for brain health purposes).

Broccoli is rich in brain-healthy nutrients like flavonoids and vitamin C

All of the suggestions we've mentioned so far can seem quite overwhelming to do in one go, particularly if it's drastically different to your current diet. The good thing is that any change is better than none. To start off with, focus on adding in those foods that are known to be beneficial to brain health and increase your consumption of those. Then, once you get on top of that, you can start to look at what foods you need to limit. You might want to start with just one new recipe a week and build from there, or maybe one meal a day.

Budget can be a concern when trying to make changes to an existing diet, which is another reason to start small. Swap out white rice for brown, or red meat for poultry. Vegetables don't always have to be organic and fresh; look for frozen or canned options too, as these are typically more cost-effective. The same goes for berries – frozen berries can be a good solution as you can just use what you need and they will last a lot longer. Wherever possible, prepare your own food at home, as this will cut out excess fat, salt and processing ingredients, while also making you more aware of what's going into your meals. Excess salt intake has been linked to high blood pressure, a risk factor for stroke, which in turn harms your brain health. Try using different herbs and spices instead to add flavour to your food.

The recipes in this book have been put together to not only be packed with brain-boosting ingredients and nutrients, but many of them are simple and quick. Start by choosing a few you like the sound of and try those first, then add in new ones over time. You'll soon learn the formula for making a healthy, balanced and brain-friendly meal, so you'll be able to pull together your own meals regularly, giving you long-term benefits.

EATING FOR A HEALTHY BRAIN

TOP 10 BRAIN BOOSTING NUTRIENTS

OMEGA-3

Found in: Fish (particularly oily fish), flaxseed oil, chia seeds

Omega is a type of polyunsaturated fatty acid that has a huge impact on brain function. There are a few types, all of which perform different jobs, including DHA, which is the most dominant omega-3 in the brain. Other common types are EPA and ALA. A paper titled 'Effects of Omega-3 Polyunsaturated Fatty Acids on Brain Functions', published in the journal *Cureus*, concluded that consumption of omega-3 improved "learning, memory ability, cognitive wellbeing and blood flow in the brain". Omega-3 should be consumed through food intake rather than supplements where possible, with fish having the highest concentrations of both DHA and EPA.

B VITAMINS

Meat (especially liver), fish, dairy products, wholewheat bread, yeast extract

There are eight different B vitamins, and we need all of them for various metabolic processes in the body. A study published in the journal *Nutrients* highlighted that we often focus on just the three best-known vitamins – B6, B9 and B12 – but for optimal brain health, we want to incorporate the full range. Another study, published in *Plos One*, found that taking high-dose B vitamin tablets (B6, B12 and folate) reduced the rate of brain shrinkage in people over 70 with mild memory problems. A varied diet is needed to consume all the B vitamins, as the foods contain different B vitamins.

GLUCOSINOLATES AND ISOTHIOCYANATES

Broccoli, kale, Brussels sprouts, cabbage, cauliflower

Glucosinolates are derived from glucose and an amino acid, whereas isothiocyanates are produced when glucosinolates are broken down. You might not be familiar with these nutrients, but they are antioxidants that protect the brain. There have been numerous studies exploring these compounds specifically looking at the potential protective effect in neurodegenerative diseases, suggesting that they may help to reduce chronic inflammation and oxidative stress.

VITAMIN E

Plant oils, sunflower seeds, spinach, peanuts, pumpkin

Vitamin E is an essential nutrient and there has been a link between people who eat a diet rich in vitamin E and a lower risk of developing dementia – specifically when deriving the vitamin from food rather than supplementation. A study from the Oregon State University has been looking at whether a vitamin E deficiency can actually cause damage to the brain, as it seemingly prevents the effective production of compounds that repair damaged membranes. It's possible to get all the vitamin E that you need through your diet, although some research suggests that in the USA, over 90% of people don't get enough dietary vitamin E.

VITAMIN C

Citrus fruits, peppers, broccoli, potatoes, berries

Concentrations of vitamin C – a powerful antioxidant – are greater in the brain than in any other part of the body. It helps neurons develop and has been shown to be an important factor in cognitive performance. A 2020 review in *BMC Psychiatry* concluded that "there is evidence suggesting that vitamin C deficiency is related to adverse mood and cognitive effects". It's also not uncommon to have a deficiency; it's estimated that about 5% of people in the UK don't get enough vitamin C, and in some parts of the world this figure can reach over 70%. It's definitely worth focusing on eating plenty of foods rich in this nutrient.

CAFFEINE

Coffee, tea, cocoa beans, matcha, guarana

In moderation, caffeine is thought to have a generally positive effect on the brain. It helps us to feel more alert and focused, and it can also improve mood. A systematic review in 2015 looking at the prevention of late-life cognitive decline and dementia, suggested that there may be some evidence that caffeine consumption, in particular coffee and tea, could offer a protective effect in the brain. It's also thought to stimulate the central nervous system, which is why you feel so awake — it blocks adenosine, the neurotransmitter that makes you feel tired. It's important to regulate your caffeine intake so that it doesn't disrupt your sleep, however.

VITAMIN K

Kale, broccoli, spinach, chicken, vegetable oils, cereal grains

Vitamin K's main purpose is to help wounds heal by clotting the blood, and it's also helpful for bone health. However, there is research to suggest that it can help with cognition too. It's thought to be associated with brain cell development and survival. A 2022 study from AlMaarefa University in Saudi Arabia looked at giving vitamin K to rats. The findings suggested that a form of vitamin K2 could be promising in terms of "halting progression of structural and cognitive deterioration in aged population". The rats in the study also showed reduced levels of depression and anxiety, as well as improved spatial memory.

MAGNESIUM

Leafy greens, avocados, legumes, tofu, nuts, dark chocolate

Magnesium could be especially beneficial to women, a 2023 study published in the *European Journal of Nutrition* suggests. The study involved over 6,000 adults in the UK supplying data that helped researchers to calculate their average daily magnesium intake. Those whose diets were richer in magnesium tended to have a greater brain volume than those who didn't, equating to a younger 'brain age' than their real age by as much as a year. And interestingly, these effects were shown to be greater in women than men. Having a larger brain volume could lead to a lower risk of dementia in later life.

FLAVONOIDS

Tea, wine, onions, soybeans, cherries

Flavonoids are a type of plant chemical (phytochemicals) that are found in a variety of fruits and vegetables. There are many different subclasses of flavonoids and different foods may have just one, or a combination of a few — which is why it's important to 'eat the rainbow' to ensure you have a wide range. It's thought that flavonoids play a key role in brain health, by reducing free radicals, which can damage cells, and having an anti-inflammatory effect. A 2009 article called 'Flavonoids and brain health', published in *Genes & Nutrition*, also found that they have the potential to "promote memory, learning and cognitive function".

POLYPHENOLS

Berries, dark chocolate, coffee, turmeric, flaxseed

There are more than 8,000 types of polyphenols across different categories, with one of them being flavonoids (listed above). Polyphenols have been widely analysed in relation to their effect on neurodegenerative disease, and also on neuroplasticity (the ability of neural networks in the brain to change) in younger people with positive results. A 2020 meta-analysis ('Effects of Polyphenol-Rich Interventions on Cognition and Brain Health in Healthy Young and Middle-Aged Adults') actually concluded that it is more advantageous to intervene at a younger age, as the effects of polyphenols seem more significant in young and middle-aged adults.

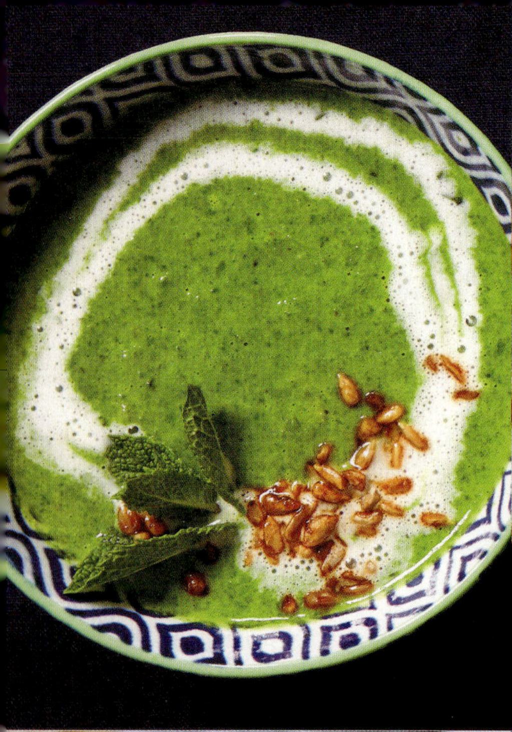
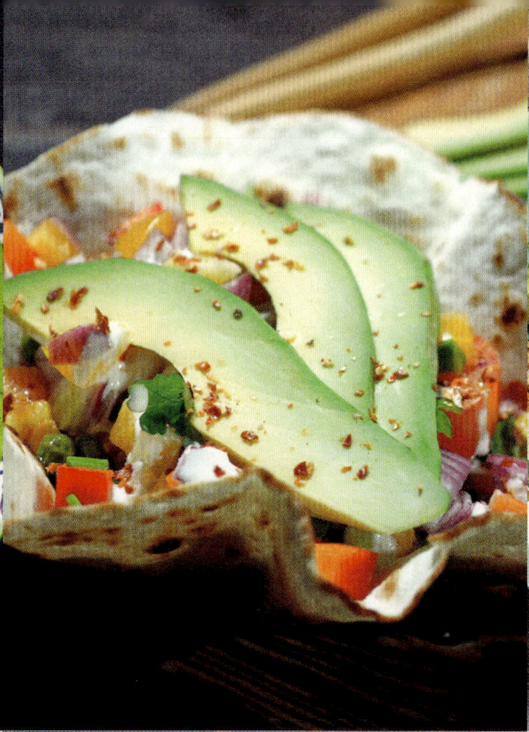
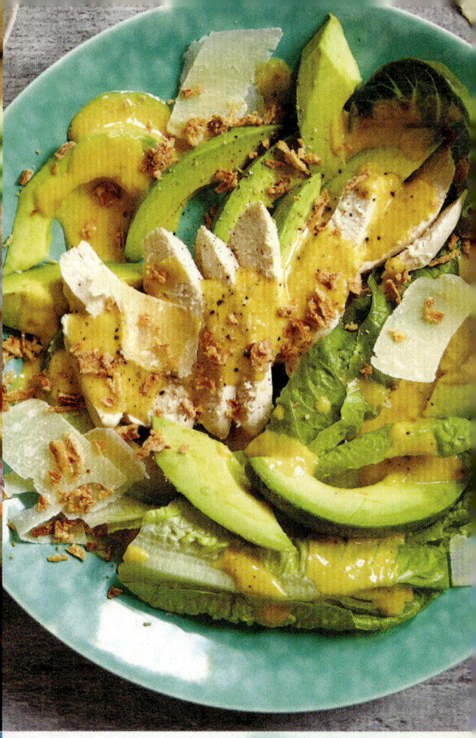
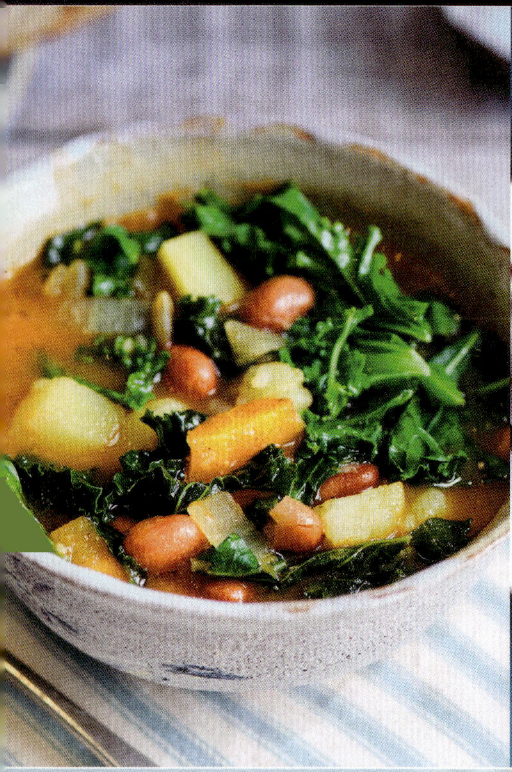
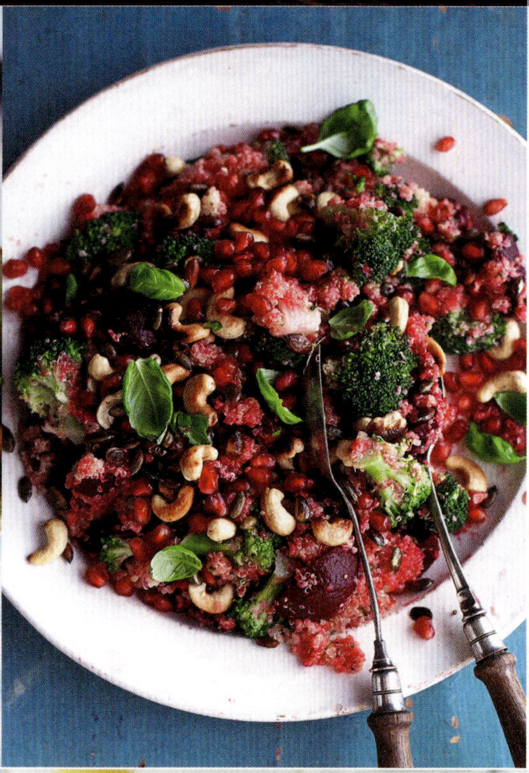
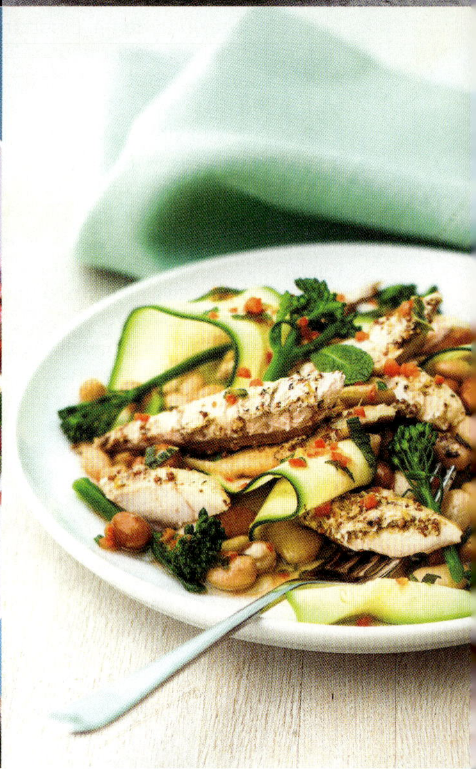
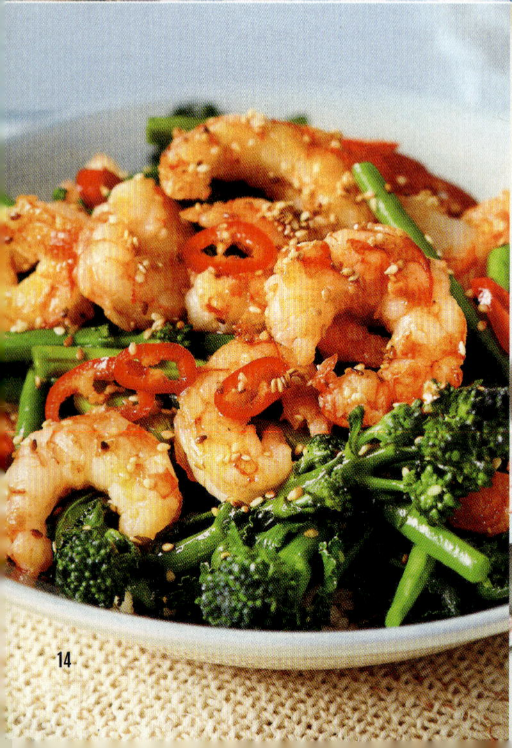
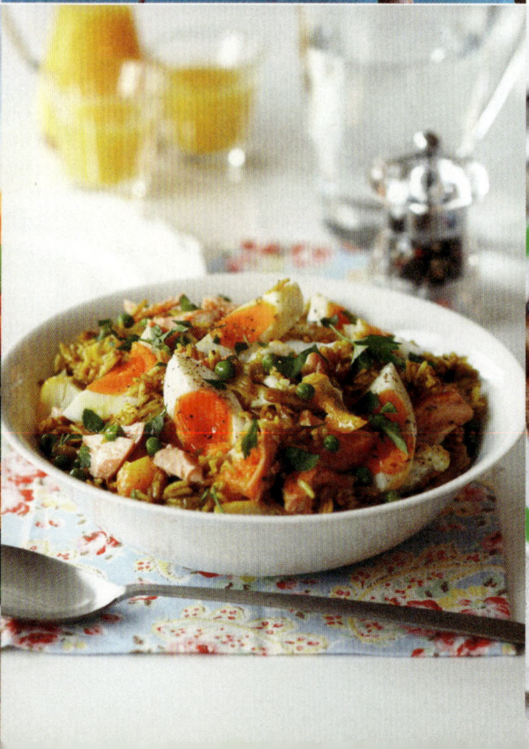
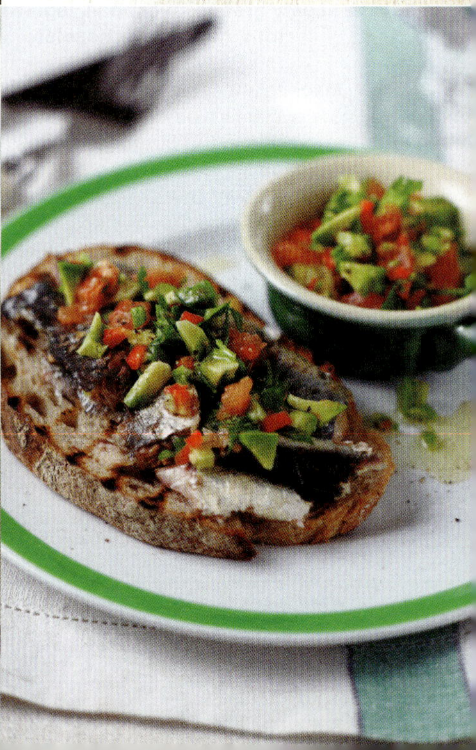

SALADS & LIGHT BITES

GREEN GODDESS SOUP	016
TACO SALAD IN TORTILLA 'BOWLS'	018
CHICKEN & AVOCADO CAESAR SALAD	020
AVOCADO, BACON, PECAN & CHICORY SALAD	022
BORLOTTI BEAN & KALE SOUP	024
HERRING SMØRREBRØD	026
MACKEREL SUPERFOOD SALAD	028
PRAWN & BROCCOLI RICE BOWL	030
CROWD-PLEASER KEDGEREE	032
SARDINES WITH AVOCADO SALSA	034
POKE BOWL	036
VEGGIE RAMEN	038
GADO GADO	040
BROCCOLI, BEET & GRAIN SALAD	042
WILD RICE SALAD WITH MISO DRESSING	044

GREEN GODDESS SOUP

A revitalising bowl of goodness – just what the doctor ordered!

SERVES 4 • READY IN 30 MINS

INGREDIENTS

- ½ tbsp olive oil
- 1 bunch spring onions, chopped
- 6 anchovies, chopped
- 2 garlic cloves, chopped
- 1 litre | 2 pints | 4 cups vegetable stock
- 200ml | 7floz | ¾ cup coconut milk
- 1 head broccoli, broken into florets
- 100g | 3.5oz frozen peas
- 2 tbsp pumpkin or sunflower seeds
- 1 tsp tamari
- 250g | 8.8oz spinach
- 1 small bunch each tarragon, basil, mint and parsley (reserve a little to serve)
- Juice of ½ lemon

METHOD

1 Heat the oil in a large pan and fry the spring onions, anchovies and garlic for a few mins. Add the stock and coconut milk (reserving a little to serve), and simmer for a few mins before adding the broccoli, then simmer for 5 mins. Add the peas and cook for 1 min, then remove from the heat.

2 To make the toasted seeds, toss the seeds with the tamari in a frying pan over a medium heat for a few mins, ensuring they don't burn. Set aside.

3 Stir the spinach through the soup until just wilted, then add the herbs and blend the soup with a stick blender until smooth. Stir through the lemon juice and top with a little coconut milk, the reserved herbs and toasted seeds to serve.

PER SERVING: CALS 224 | FAT 15G | SAT FAT 8.5G | CARBS 9G

MAKE IT VEGGIE

Simply use 3 tbsp of capers instead of the anchovies if you want to make it vegetarian. The anchovies do add a nice depth to the flavour and are also a great source of omega-3 along with other key nutrients.

SALADS & LIGHT BITES

TACO SALAD IN TORTILLA 'BOWLS'

SALADS & LIGHT BITES

TACO SALAD IN TORTILLA 'BOWLS'

A fresh and light dish with brain-healthy avocado

SERVES 2 • READY IN 20 MINS

INGREDIENTS

- 2 large wholemeal tortillas
- 1 avocado, stoned, peeled and sliced
- ½ red onion, diced finely
- 2 large tomatoes, diced
- 2 tbsp cooked sweetcorn
- 1x 400g | 14oz tin black beans, drained and rinsed
- ½ red pepper, diced finely
- 1 lime, zested and juiced
- 1 tsp chilli flakes
- 2 tbsp fresh coriander, chopped finely
- Olive oil

METHOD

1 Preheat the oven to 200°C (180°C fan) | 390°F | Gas 6. Turn a large muffin tin upside down and lightly grease with olive oil. Place each tortilla between the domes of the muffin moulds, and shape into bowls. Place in the oven to bake for 10 mins, then remove and leave to cool.

2 In a large bowl, mix together the red onion, tomatoes, sweetcorn, black beans, pepper, lime zest, fresh coriander and chilli flakes with approximately 1 tbsp olive oil.

3 Spoon the taco mixture into the tortilla bowls, and top with the avocado to serve.

PER SERVING: CALS 750 | FAT 18g | SAT FAT 4.5g | CARBS 16g

CHEF'S TIP
To turn this salad into something more substantial, you could add some cooked wholegrain rice or quinoa to the filling mixture.

CHICKEN & AVOCADO CAESAR SALAD

CHICKEN & AVOCADO CAESAR SALAD

Add some extra brain-boosting nutrients to the classic Caesar salad by including some vitamin-packed avocados

SERVES 4 • READY IN 10 MINS

INGREDIENTS

FOR THE DRESSING

- 2 eggs yolks
- 4 anchovy fillets, optional
- ½ tsp mustard powder
- 1 tbsp red wine vinegar
- 150ml | 5floz | ½ cup extra-virgin olive oil
- 2 tbsp Parmesan, finely shaved

FOR THE SALAD

- 1 head of romaine lettuce or 2 cos heads, roughly chopped
- 2 cooked chicken breasts, sliced
- 2 avocados, sliced
- 1 tbsp crispy fried onions

METHOD

1 For the dressing, put all the ingredients except the oil and Parmesan into a food processor and whizz until smooth. With the motor running, gradually add the oil until you have a smooth dressing. Stir in the Parmesan and set aside - this will keep in the fridge for three days.

2 Toss together the lettuce, chicken and avocado, and stir through the dressing. Top with the crispy fried onions and serve.

PER SERVING: CALS 598 | FAT 51G | SAT FAT 10G | CARBS 4G

MAKE IT VEGGIE

Substitute the anchovies for some capers or even some chopped black olives to make this salad meat-free without sacrificing depth of flavour. You can omit the Parmesan or swap it for a vegetarian or vegan alternative.

SALADS & LIGHT BITES

AVOCADO, BACON, PECAN & CHICORY SALAD

SALADS & LIGHT BITES

AVOCADO, BACON, PECAN & CHICORY SALAD

We love this salad as a lunch but it works perfectly for dinner, too

SERVES 4 • READY IN 15 MINS

INGREDIENTS

FOR THE SALAD

200g | 7oz smoked streaky bacon or pancetta, thinly sliced and cut in half

2 heads of chicory, leaves separated

3 avocados, halved and sliced

50g | 1.8oz pecan nuts, thinly sliced

FOR THE DRESSING

5 tbsp avocado oil

1 tbsp white wine vinegar

1 shallot, finely sliced

2 tsp wholegrain mustard

METHOD

1 In two batches, dry-fry the streaky bacon or pancetta in a pan until crisp.

2 Put all the chicory leaves in a salad bowl, then top with the avocado, bacon or pancetta, and pecans.

3 For the dressing, whisk together all the ingredients in a small bowl with 1 tbsp water. Season to taste. Spoon over the salad just before serving.

PER SERVING: CALS 600 | FAT 57G | SAT FAT 11G | CARBS 7G

MAKE IT VEGGIE

You could use a meat-free bacon substitute, or swap the bacon for some small cubes of tofu fried until crispy.

BORLOTTI BEAN & KALE SOUP

SALADS & LIGHT BITES

BORLOTTI BEAN & KALE SOUP

This is light yet filling, making it perfect for any time of year. The kale is a great veg source of omega-3s

SERVES 8 • READY IN 30 MINS

INGREDIENTS

1 tbsp olive oil

1 onion, diced

1 large carrot (approx 200g | 7oz), diced

1 large potato (approx 350g | 12.3oz), cut into small chunks

1 tbsp tomato puree

Few fresh thyme sprigs

2 bay leaves

1ltr | 2pt | 4 cups hot vegetable or chicken stock

400g | 14oz tin of borlotti beans, drained and rinsed

125g | 4.4oz kale, chopped (remove any tough stems)

METHOD

1 Heat the oil in a large pan. Add the onion and carrot and cook over a medium heat for about 5 mins.

2 Add the potato, tomato puree, thyme and bay leaves, stir well for 2 mins and then pour in the stock. Bring to the boil, then simmer gently for about 10 mins, partially covered.

3 Stir in the borlotti beans and add seasoning. Bring back to the boil, then put the kale on top and let it steam for 5 mins. Spoon into warmed bowls and serve.

PER SERVING: CALS 86 | FAT 2g | SAT FAT 0.5g | CARBS 11g

CHEF'S TIP
Stretch the soup even further by adding some chopped celery stalks, and/or 2 chopped turnips. Add some garlic or any type of beans you like. For a meaty version, you could add crispy bacon, pancetta or cooked ham.

HERRING SMØRREBRØD

SALADS & LIGHT BITES

HERRING SMØRREBRØD

A classic Danish, open-faced sandwich, perfect for lunch or a light summer supper

SERVES 4 • READY IN 20 MINS

INGREDIENTS

FOR THE CUCUMBER PICKLE
4 tbsp white wine vinegar
1 tsp salt
2 tbsp caster sugar
1 tsp mustard seeds
2 star anise
Bay leaf
1 cucumber, thinly sliced

FOR THE BEETROOT DIP
4 cooked beetroot
75g | 2.6oz walnuts, lightly toasted
1 tbsp horseradish sauce
1 tbsp pomegranate molasses
Juice of ½ a lemon
1 clove garlic
4 tbsp crème fraîche
½ tsp sumac

FOR THE SMØRREBRØD
8 slices rye bread
240g | 8.5oz jar herrings, drained
1 bunch dill

METHOD

1 To make the pickle, heat the vinegar with the salt, sugar, mustard seeds, star anise and bay leaf. Once the sugar has dissolved, remove from the heat and stir in the sliced cucumber. Set aside to marinate and cool.

2 To make the dip, blend ingredients in a food processor and season well.

3 To assemble the smørrebrød, spread 2 tbsp beetroot dip on each slice of rye bread, then top with herring, pickle, fresh dill sprigs and extra crème fraîche, if you like.

PER SERVING: CALS 514 | FAT 24G | SAT FAT 5.5G | CARBS 51G

REDUCE WASTE
The leftover beetroot dip will keep for 3 days in the fridge. You could serve it alongside crudités, or use it as a sandwich spread.

MACKEREL SUPERFOOD SALAD

SALADS & LIGHT BITES

MACKEREL SUPERFOOD SALAD

Mackerel is another oily fish hero that is packed with beneficial omega-3s

SERVES 4 • READY IN 20 MINS

INGREDIENTS

3 tbsp wholegrain mustard
4 tsp olive oil
Zest and juice of 1 lemon
4 mackerel fillets
125g | 4.4oz pack Tenderstem broccoli tips
400g | 14oz can mixed bean salad, drained and rinsed
Small handful of chopped mint, some reserved for garnish
2 courgettes, finely sliced lengthways with a peeler
1 red chilli, finely diced, some reserved for garnish
2 tbsp red wine vinegar

METHOD

1 Heat the grill to medium. In a bowl mix together the mustard, 2 tsp oil, the lemon zest and juice.

2 Put the mackerel on a wire rack and cover with two-thirds of the mustard paste. Grill for 2 mins on each side, cool a little, then flake.

3 Meanwhile, cook the broccoli for 3 mins, then drain.

4 Gently mix the beans with the mint, courgettes, most of the chilli, remaining oil, remaining mustard paste and vinegar.

5 Arrange the beans, courgette and mackerel on plates and garnish with mint and chilli.

PER SERVING: CALS 349 | FAT 22g | SAT FAT 4g | CARBS 6g

CHEF'S TIP

Look for line-caught mackerel where possible, for a more sustainable choice.

PHOTO: FUTURECONTENTHUB.COM

PRAWN & BROCCOLI RICE BOWL

PRAWN & BROCCOLI RICE BOWL

A tasty, quick meal with a zingy sesame dressing. Prawns are an excellent source of vitamin B12, which aids energy production and cognition

SERVES 4 • READY IN 20 MINS

INGREDIENTS

A little oil, for frying
300g | 10.5oz peeled, raw king prawns, defrosted
400g | 14oz Tenderstem broccoli, trimmed
200g | 7oz fine green beans, trimmed
250g | 8.8oz microwave wholegrain rice
1 tbsp sesame seeds, toasted
1 red chilli, sliced

FOR THE DRESSING
2 tbsp sesame oil
2 tbsp soy sauce
2 tbsp rice wine vinegar
1 tbsp honey

METHOD

1 Heat the oil in a pan and cook the prawns for a few mins until pink and cooked through. Steam the broccoli and beans for 5 mins until tender. Heat the rice in the microwave, following the pack instructions.

2 Mix together all of the dressing ingredients. Toss the broccoli, beans and rice in the dressing with half the sesame seeds. Top with the cooked prawns and scatter over the red chilli and remaining sesame seeds.

PER SERVING: CALS 343 | FAT 16.5g | SAT FAT 3g | CARBS 42g

REDUCE WASTE
Any leftovers are great served cold for lunch the next day.

SALADS & LIGHT BITES

CROWD-PLEASER KEDGEREE

SALADS & LIGHT BITES

CROWD-PLEASER KEDGEREE

Kedgeree, the classic dish of smoked fish and rice, is a warming family meal rich in protein and brimming with vital vitamins and minerals

SERVES 4 • READY IN 25 MINS

INGREDIENTS

- 4 medium free-range eggs
- 1 tbsp olive oil
- 150g | 5.3oz skinless smoked haddock fillet
- 1 tbsp mild curry paste (such as korma)
- 300ml | 10floz | 1¼ cups hot vegetable stock
- 2x 250g | 8.8oz pouches microwave basmati rice
- 125g | 4.4oz frozen peas
- 150g | 5.3oz hot smoked salmon, flaked
- 3 tbsp parsley, chopped

METHOD

1 Put the eggs in a pan, cover with cold water, bring to the boil and simmer for 4 mins. Plunge the eggs into cold water to cool.

2 While the eggs are cooking, heat the oil in a large frying pan. Add the smoked haddock and cook for 8-10 mins, turning once, until opaque and flakes easily. Remove from the pan and set aside on a plate.

3 Add the curry paste to the pan with half the stock. Stir in the rice and simmer, stirring occasionally, for 5 mins.

4 Flake the haddock into chunks, add to the pan with the peas, salmon and remaining stock. Cook for 3 mins to heat through. Peel the eggs and cut into quarters. Stir in the parsley and top with the soft-boiled eggs. Season and serve.

PER SERVING: CALS 464 | FAT 19g | SAT FAT 4g | CARBS 39g

FOOD FOR THOUGHT
Haddock is a great low-fat, source of protein, while salmon is one of the best sources of the fatty acid DHA.

SARDINES WITH AVOCADO SALSA

SALADS & LIGHT BITES

SARDINES WITH AVOCADO SALSA

This fish, eaten bones and all, is an excellent source of calcium

SERVES 2 • READY IN 15 MINS

INGREDIENTS

120g | 4.2oz tin sardines in oil
4 slices sourdough bread

FOR THE SALSA
1 ripe avocado
½ small red onion, finely chopped
4 tomatoes, deseeded and chopped
½ red chilli, deseeded and chopped
Juice ½ lime
1 tbsp fresh coriander, chopped

METHOD

1 Make the salsa first, peel the avocado and remove the stone. Dice the flesh and place in a bowl with the red onion, tomatoes, red chilli, lime juice and coriander. Season to taste.

2 Drain the sardines and break them up a little using a fork. Toast the sourdough bread, then place the sardines on top and serve topped with the salsa.

PER SERVING: CALS 517 | FAT 23g | SAT FAT 5g | CARBS 51g

FOOD FOR THOUGHT
A can of sardines contributes around 6µg vitamin D to an adult's daily requirement of 15-20µg.

POKE BOWL

POKE BOWL

This delicious lunch bowl is filled with anti-inflammatory ingredients

SERVES 4 • READY IN 35 MINS + 1 HR MARINATING

INGREDIENTS

300g | 11oz tofu, extra firm
2 tbsp soy sauce
Lime juice from 1 lime
1 tbsp sesame oil
2 tsp ginger paste
200g | 7oz brown rice, cooked and cooled
2 medium carrots, grated
100g | 4oz edamame beans, cooked
2 avocados, halved and sliced
200g | 7oz tinned sweetcorn, drained
Handful of microgreens

TO GARNISH
Sesame seeds
Handful of fresh coriander

METHOD

1 Cut the tofu up into 2.5cm | 1" squares.

2 Add the soy sauce, lime juice, sesame oil and ginger paste into a medium bowl and then whisk together. Add the cubed tofu to the bowl and coat with the sauce. Put to one side to marinate for at least an hour.

3 Cook the rice and edamame beans (if frozen) according to the instructions on the packet.

4 Grate the carrots. Fill bowls with rice then add the remaining ingredients in sections over it. Drizzle any remaining marinade. Garnish with sesame seeds and coriander.

PER SERVING: CALS 707 | FAT 27g | SAT FAT 5.4g | CARBS 8.4g

FOOD FOR THOUGHT
Edamame beans are rich in isoflavones, which may help reduce the risk of cognitive decline in old age.

SALADS & LIGHT BITES

VEGGIE RAMEN

LOW IN SATURATED FAT AND SALT

SALADS & LIGHT BITES

VEGGIE RAMEN

A wholesome broth packed with goodness – mushrooms are rich in brain-supporting vitamin D

SERVES 2 • READY IN 30 MINS

INGREDIENTS

200g | 7oz aubergine, cut into chunks
2 tsp olive oil
200g | 7oz mixed mushrooms, sliced
200g | 7oz marinated, smoked or regular tofu, cubed
4 sachets miso soup paste, or 4 tbsp miso paste
160g | 5.6oz ramen noodles
150g | 5.3oz Tenderstem broccoli
200g | 7oz soya beans
2 tsp pre-chopped ginger, or a thumb-sized piece of fresh ginger, chopped
2 tbsp soy sauce
200g | 7oz radishes, sliced
Handful fresh watercress or salad leaves

METHOD

1 In a large non-stick pan, lightly fry the chunks of aubergine in the oil. Once tender, add the mushrooms and fry until soft and golden. Add the tofu to heat through.

2 Meanwhile, put the miso soup paste into a pan with 1.2ltr | 2.5pt boiling water. Add the noodles and broccoli, and cook until just tender.

3 Add the aubergine and tofu mixture, soya beans and the lazy ginger, then stir through some soy sauce, to taste. Heat through, then serve in bowls topped with slices of radish and watercress or salad leaves.

PER SERVING: CALS 400 | FAT 15g | SAT FAT 2g | CARBS 46g

CHEF'S TIP

Like it spicy? Include some freshly chopped red chillies for an extra kick and added vitamins. You could also swap the tofu for some chopped chicken breast for a non-veggie version.

RECIPE AND PHOTO: FUTURECONTENTHUB.COM

GADO GADO

GADO GADO

Tofu is a great source of protein and calcium for those on dairy-free diets

SERVES 6 • READY IN 40 MINS

INGREDIENTS

500g | 1.1lb sweet potatoes, cubed
1 courgette, cubed
1 red pepper, deseeded and chopped
1 cauliflower, cut into florets
2 garlic cloves, crushed
4 tbsp olive oil
200g | 7oz green beans
200g | 7oz marinated tofu
1 small bunch coriander, chopped
60g | 2oz salted peanuts, chopped, to serve
Lime wedges, to serve

FOR THE PEANUT DRESSING

1 tbsp sunflower oil
1 red onion, chopped
4 garlic cloves, chopped
1 red chilli, deseeded and chopped
1 tsp tamari or soy sauce
4 lime leaves, chopped
250ml | 8.5floz coconut cream
225g | 8oz jar crunchy peanut butter

METHOD

1 Heat the oven to 200°C (180°C fan) | 390°F | gas 6. Spread the sweet potatoes, courgette and red pepper out in a roasting tin. Spread the cauliflower out in another tin. Sprinkle the garlic over the veg and drizzle with oil. Roast for 25 mins, then cool.

2 To make the peanut dressing, heat the oil in a pan and fry the red onion for a few mins, to soften. Add the garlic and chilli. Cook for 1 min, then add the rest of the dressing ingredients and 150ml | 5floz | ⅔ cup boiling water. Stir until smooth and leave to cool.

3 Cook the green beans with 2 tbsp water on High in the microwave for 3 mins. Drain and rinse under cold water to cool them quickly.

4 Divide the dressing between 6 bowls. Spoon on the cooled roasted veg, beans and tofu. Sprinkle with coriander and peanuts. Serve with lime wedges.

PER SERVING: CALS 715 | FAT 49g | SAT FAT 15g | CARBS 36g

FOOD FOR THOUGHT

Tofu is high in calcium, which helps control blood flow to the brain.

SALADS & LIGHT BITES

BROCCOLI, BEET & GRAIN SALAD

SALADS & LIGHT BITES

BROCCOLI, BEET & GRAIN SALAD

Adding grains to a simple salad will transform it from a light lunch to a more substantial evening meal

SERVES 4 • READY IN 25 MINS

INGREDIENTS

- 60g | 2oz cashew nuts
- 30g | 1oz pumpkin seeds
- 1ltr | 2pt | 4 cups vegetable stock
- 200g | 7oz quinoa or brown rice
- 360g | 12.7oz broccoli, cut into florets
- 250g | 8.8oz cooked beetroot, drained and quartered
- Balsamic vinegar

METHOD

1 In a small pan, toast the nuts and seeds, mix regularly until lightly browned.

2 Meanwhile, bring the stock to a boil. Add the quinoa or rice. Simmer for 10 mins, before adding the broccoli and cooking for 5 more mins. Drain and tip into a serving dish.

3 Stir in the beetroot, toasted nuts and seeds. Season, then serve, either warm or cold, drizzled with balsamic vinegar.

PER SERVING: CALS 370 | FAT 14g | SAT FAT 2g | CARBS 39g

FOOD FOR THOUGHT
Seeds and nuts bring flavour, texture and brain-healthy monounsaturated fats.

WILD RICE SALAD WITH MISO DRESSING

Kick off your meal in style with wild rice and an umami miso dressing

SERVES 4 • READY IN 45 MINS

INGREDIENTS

FOR THE DRESSING

- 2 tbsp white miso paste
- 2 tbsp mild-flavoured honey
- 4cm | 1½" fresh ginger, peeled and finely grated
- 2 tbsp soy sauce
- Juice of 2 limes

FOR THE SALAD

- 400g | 14oz pumpkin or squash, peeled and cut into 2cm | ¾" cubes
- 2 tbsp olive oil
- 175g | 6oz wild rice
- 100g | 3.5oz frozen edamame (soya) beans, defrosted
- 1 head red chicory, trimmed and leaves separated
- 4 spring onions, shredded
- 1 avocado, stoned and diced
- 2 tbsp pumpkin seeds

METHOD

1 To make the dressing, simply whisk all the ingredients together and keep in the fridge until needed (it will keep in an airtight container for a week).

2 Heat the oven to 190°C (170°C fan) | 375°F | gas 5. Toss the pumpkin or squash with the olive oil, season well and spread out on a baking sheet. Roast for about 30 mins until soft and turning brown. Set aside to cool.

3 Meanwhile, rinse the rice in a sieve, put in a pan and cover with 350ml | 11.8floz | 1½ cups water, add a good pinch of salt and bring to the boil. Cover, reduce the heat and simmer for about 30 mins, until the rice is plump and soft; add a little extra water if it appears to be drying out at any point.

4 Add the edamame beans to the rice and leave to cool. Gently fold the rice, beans and remaining ingredients together with the dressing and serve.

PER SERVING: CALS 400 | FAT 16G | SAT FAT 16G | CARBS 48G

FOOD FOR THOUGHT

Fermented foods like miso may boost brain health by supporting the gut-brain axis.

SALADS & LIGHT BITES

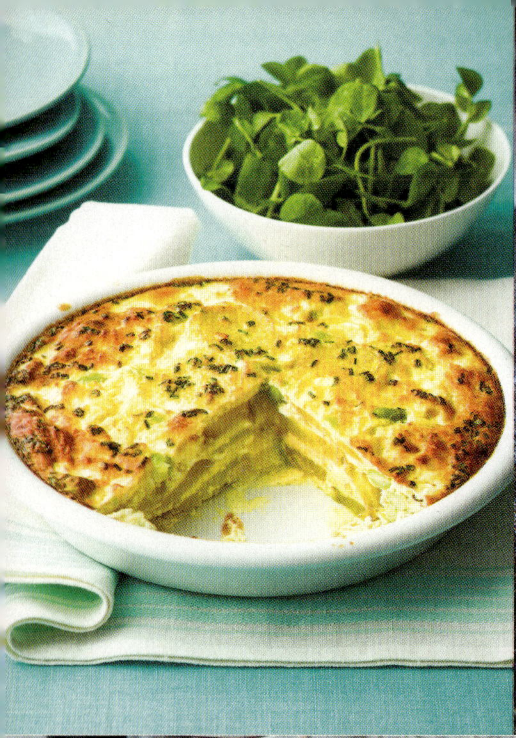
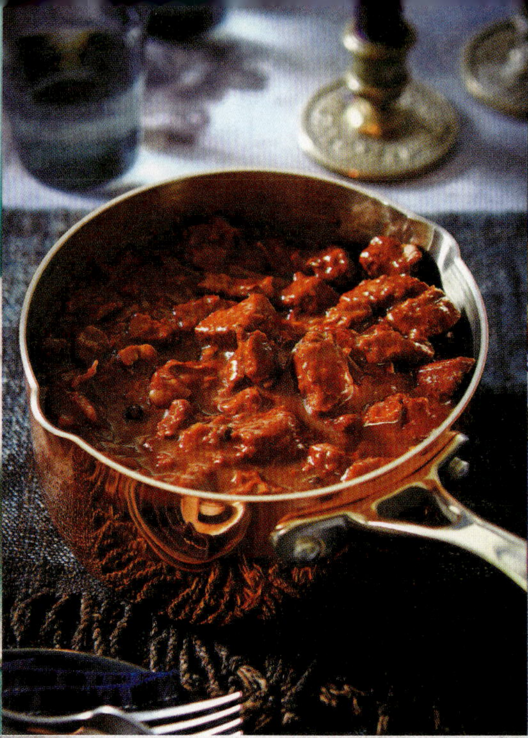
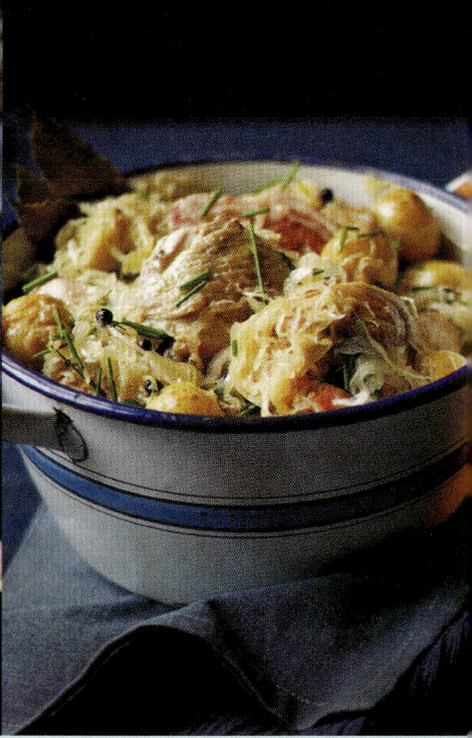
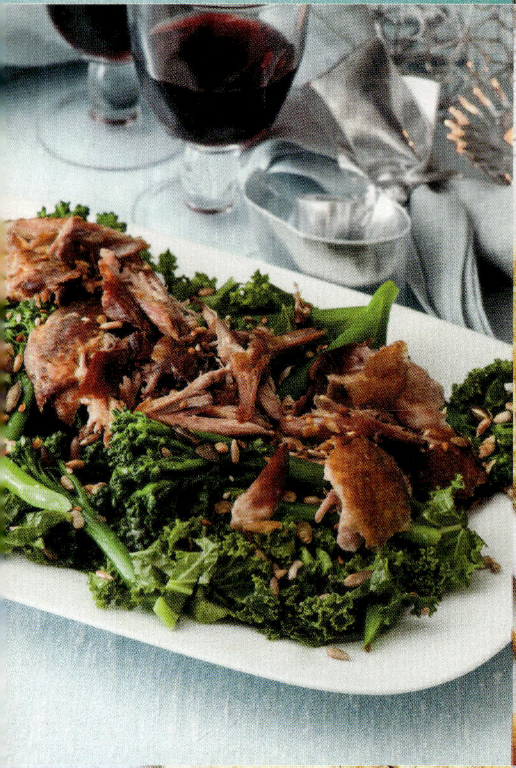
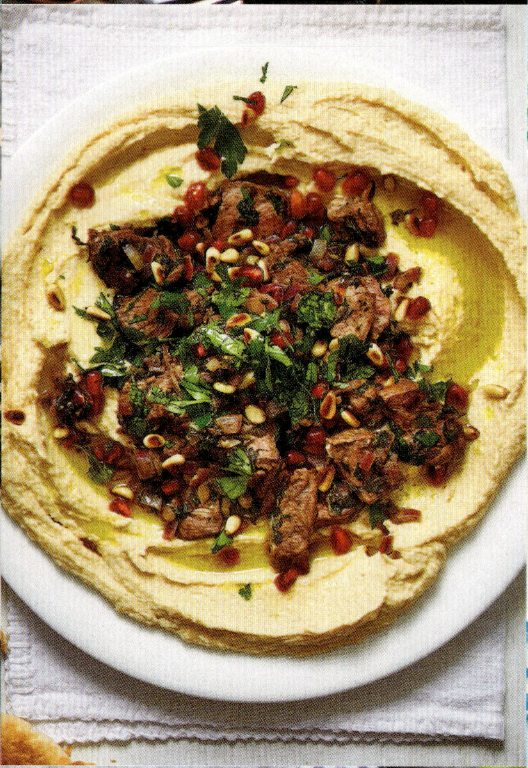
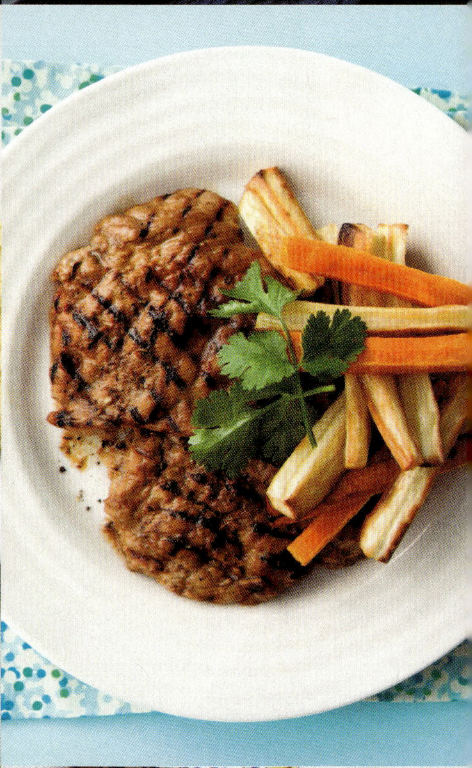
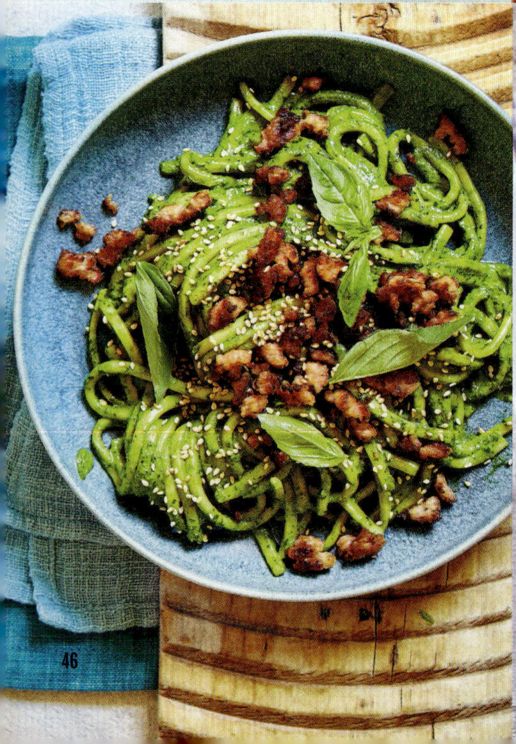
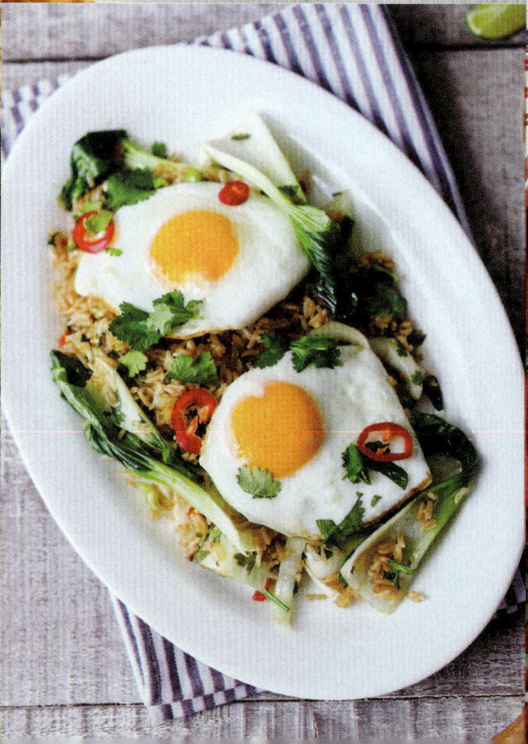
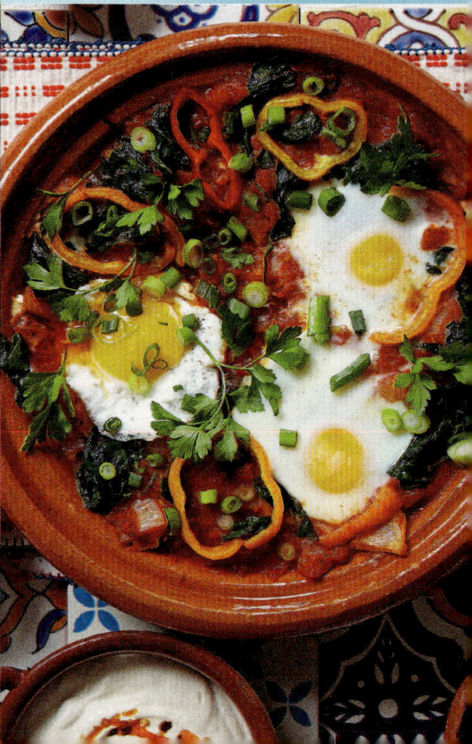

MEAT, POULTRY & VEG

ROSEMARY, CRANBERRY, JUNIPER & BEEF CASSEROLE 048

CHICKEN STEW WITH SAUERKRAUT 050

DUCK & HEALTHY GREENS SALAD 052

FLAXSEED HOUMOUS & SPICED LAMB 054

MISO PORK WITH ROOT VEGETABLE CHIPS 056

WALNUT & SESAME PESTO PASTA WITH CRISPY SAUSAGE 058

AROMATIC FRIED RICE & EGGS 060

SPICY TURKISH EGGS WITH TAHINI YOGURT 062

EDAMAME, COTTAGE CHEESE & NEW POTATO FRITTATA 064

SUPER-GREENS VEG & TOFU STIR-FRY 066

TOFU SKEWERS & NOODLE SALAD 068

ROSEMARY, CRANBERRY, JUNIPER & BEEF CASSEROLE

This rich beef casserole is the perfect winter comfort food, full of familiar flavours and tender meat

SERVES 6 • READY IN 2-3 HOURS

INGREDIENTS

200g | 7oz smoked lardons
1 onion, diced
3 garlic cloves, crushed
1 tbsp olive oil
1.2kg | 2.6lb braising beef, diced
45g | 1.5oz flour
300ml | 10floz | 1¼ cups red wine
450ml | 15.2floz | scant 2 cups beef stock
250g | 8.8oz redcurrant jelly
1 tsp juniper berries
5 sprigs rosemary
Steamed vegetables and mashed potatoes, to serve

METHOD

1 Heat the oven to 150°C (130°C fan) | 300°F | gas 2. In a large pan, fry the lardons until crisp. Remove and set aside. Add the onion, garlic and oil and cook for a few mins, until soft. Remove and set aside.

2 Dust the beef in the flour and season well. Fry in batches, in the same pan, until browned. Add the onion, garlic, lardons and remaining ingredients to the pan.

3 Cover and move to the oven. Cook for 2-3 hrs, until the meat is tender. Serve with vegetables and potatoes.

PER SERVING: CALS 480 | FAT 12g | SAT FAT 4g | CARBS 33g

CHEF'S TIP
You could also enjoy this stew with venison shoulder instead of the beef.

MEAT, POULTRY & VEG

CHICKEN STEW WITH SAUERKRAUT

MEAT, POULTRY & VEG

CHICKEN STEW WITH SAUERKRAUT

Pickled and fermented foods like sauerkraut have been found to be good for your gut, which may in turn help your brain, too. Sauerkraut is also almost all fibre, which helps you feel fuller for longer

SERVES 6 • READY IN 1 HR

INGREDIENTS

1 tbsp oil
6 chicken drumsticks
6 chicken thighs
1 large leek, cut into thick rounds
8 rashers of smoked bacon, diced
1.3kg | 2.9lb prepared sauerkraut (around 2 jars), drained
4 bay leaves
1 tbsp juniper berries, lightly crushed
2 tsp peppercorns
275ml | 9.3floz | 1⅛ cup Polish beer – such as Tyskie
400g | 14oz small new potatoes, scrubbed
Snipped chives, to serve

METHOD

1 Heat the oil in a large, lidded flameproof casserole, add the chicken drumsticks and thighs in batches and brown well on all sides, then remove to a plate. Add the leek and bacon to the casserole and fry for 5 mins.

2 Return the chicken to the casserole. Add the sauerkraut, bay, juniper berries, peppercorns, lager (or beer) and potatoes. Season and bring to the boil, then cover and simmer for 35-40 mins, or until the chicken is cooked through and the potatoes are tender. Scatter over the chives. Serve with mustard, gherkins and rye bread, if you like.

PER SERVING: CALS 390 | FAT 17g | SAT FAT 2g | CARBS 14g

CHEF'S TIP
Replace the beer with the same volume of chicken or vegetable stock for a non-alcoholic version.

DUCK & HEALTHY GREENS SALAD

FOOD FOR THOUGHT

Broccoli contains glucosinolates, which when processed by the body can help reduce oxidative stress.

MEAT, POULTRY & VEG

DUCK & HEALTHY GREENS SALAD

Think Chinese-style crispy duck with a punchy Asian dressing and crunchy greens – a lighter version of a rich classic

SERVES 6 • READY IN 2 HRS 45 MINS

INGREDIENTS

4 duck legs
150ml | 5floz | ⅔ cup soy sauce
7.5cm | 3" piece of root ginger, roughly chopped
4 garlic cloves, bruised
2 star anise
1 cinnamon stick

FOR THE SALAD
300g | 10.6oz Tenderstem broccoli
300g | 10.6oz kale, shredded
4 tbsp mixed seeds, lightly toasted

FOR THE DRESSING
2 tbsp sweet miso paste
1 tbsp toasted sesame oil
Juice of 2 limes

METHOD

1 Put the duck skin side down in a deep pan and pour over the soy sauce and enough water to cover. Add the ginger, garlic, star anise and cinnamon, cover with a lid and bring to the boil. Reduce the heat to a simmer and cook for 30 mins. Turn the duck legs over and continue poaching for 1-1½ hours or until tender. Remove from the heat and set aside to cool, then remove from the cooking liquor and pat dry.

2 Meanwhile, bring a pan of water to the boil, cook the broccoli for two minutes then rinse in cold water and set aside. Put the kale in a large bowl, cover with boiling water and leave for a minute. Drain, rinse under cold water, and then set aside.

3 Heat the oven to 200°C (180°C fan) | 400°F | gas 6. Put the duck in the oven, skin side up, for 20 to 30 mins, until crisp. Shred while hot. Combine the dressing ingredients until smooth, then toss with the kale, broccoli, shredded duck and seeds.

PER SERVING: CALS 294 | FAT 15g | SAT FAT 3g | CARBS 11g

FLAXSEED HOUMOUS & SPICED LAMB

Flaxseed and grass-fed lamb are both excellent sources of omega-3s. This speedy recipe transforms houmous into a delicious main meal

SERVES 2 • READY IN 30 MINS

INGREDIENTS

FOR THE LAMB
½ tsp cinnamon
1 tsp allspice
1 tsp za'atar
Juice of half a lemon
200g | 7oz lamb neck, chopped into 2.5cm | 1" pieces
1 onion, chopped

FOR THE HOUMOUS
400g | 14oz tin chickpeas, drained, water reserved
2 tbsp tahini
Juice 1 lemon
1 garlic clove, crushed
120g | 4.2oz flaxseed (ground linseed)

TO SERVE (OPTIONAL)
Half a bunch each fresh mint and parsley, chopped
50g | 1.8oz pomegranate seeds
2 tbsp toasted pine nuts
4 small, toasted pitta breads or flatbreads

METHOD

1 In a bowl, mix all the marinade ingredients with the lamb and onion, cover and leave in the fridge for at least 4 hours or ideally overnight.

2 For the houmous, blitz the chickpeas, half the reserved water, tahini, lemon juice and garlic in a food processor until smooth. Add the flaxseed and more water as needed to reach a smooth consistency. Season and set aside.

3 Heat some olive oil in a frying pan and add the onion. Soften for 3-4 mins, then add the lamb and marinade, and fry for a further 8-10 mins, until the meat is cooked through.

4 Serve the lamb on top of a large dish of the houmous, and scatter with chopped mint and parsley, pomegranate seeds, toasted pine nuts and a good drizzle of olive oil, with the toasted pitta breads or flatbreads on the side.

PER SERVING: CALS 828 | FAT 58g | SAT FAT 10g | CARBS 30g

REDUCE WASTE
This houmous makes an excellent snack for packed lunches.

MEAT, POULTRY & VEG

MISO PORK WITH ROOT VEGETABLE CHIPS

MEAT, POULTRY & VEG

MISO PORK WITH ROOT VEGETABLE CHIPS

This salty, moreish miso marinade would also work brilliantly with chicken

SERVES 2 • READY IN 25 MINS

INGREDIENTS

**2 medium carrots, peeled
2 medium parsnips, peeled
1 tbsp olive oil
200g | 7oz pork fillet
1 tbsp white miso paste
1 tbsp rice vinegar
Coriander leaves, to garnish**

METHOD

1 Heat the oven to 200°C (180°C fan) | 390°F | gas 6. Cut the carrots and parsnips into chips, brush with the oil and roast in the oven for 20 minutes.

2 Meanwhile, slice the pork fillet crossways into 2 and bash with a rolling pin to make 2 thin escalopes.

3 Coat the pork with the miso paste and vinegar. Cook on a griddle for 15 minutes. Serve with the chips and garnish with coriander.

PER SERVING: CALS 338 | FAT 12g | SAT FAT 2.5g | CARBS 31g

CHEF'S TIP

You can find white miso paste in most large supermarkets, where it's usually located in the world foods aisle.

WALNUT & SESAME PESTO PASTA WITH CRISPY SAUSAGE

WALNUT & SESAME PESTO PASTA WITH CRISPY SAUSAGE

Walnuts provide a healthy dose of omega-3s. Leafy greens like spinach are also a great source of these healthy fatty acids, so this twist on classic pesto delivers great nutritional bang for your buck

SERVES 6 • READY IN 25 MINS

INGREDIENTS

- 350g | 12.3oz baby spinach
- Small bunch coriander, including stems
- Small bunch basil, including stems
- 50g | 1.8oz walnuts, lightly toasted
- 1 garlic clove, crushed
- 5 tbsp avocado or olive oil
- 1 tbsp toasted sesame oil (optional)
- Juice 1 lemon
- 500g | 17.6oz long pasta (we used bucatini)
- 4 sausages, casing removed
- Sesame seeds, to garnish, optional

METHOD

1 In a blender, blitz the spinach, coriander, basil, miso, garlic, oils and lemon juice. Add 2 tbsp water to loosen if necessary.

2 Cook the pasta according to the pack instructions.

3 Cook the sausage meat in a frying pan on a medium-high heat, stirring to break up, until crispy.

4 Toss the noodles in the pesto and top with sausage, and if using, sesame seeds.

PER SERVING: CALS 560 | FAT 25g | SAT FAT 5g | CARBS 63g

FOOD FOR THOUGHT

Avocado oil is high in omega-3s, along with a host of nutrients.

MEAT, POULTRY & VEG

AROMATIC FRIED RICE & EGGS

CHEF'S TIP
If you would like some extra protein, this recipe would also be great with the addition of some chicken breast, prawns or tofu.

MEAT, POULTRY & VEG

AROMATIC FRIED RICE & EGGS

Omega-3-enriched eggs are really good for upping the intake in your diet, particularly for vegetarians and those who don't eat fish

SERVES 2 • READY IN 20 MINS

INGREDIENTS

1 tbsp extra virgin olive oil, plus 2 tsp for frying the eggs

1 small onion, halved and sliced thinly

2 garlic cloves, crushed

2 tsp grated fresh ginger

2 red chillies, sliced

2 omega-3-enriched eggs

250g | 9oz cooked basmati rice

2 tsp soy sauce

½ tsp fish sauce

2 pak choi, roughly chopped

4 spring onions, sliced

Large handful of coriander, roughly chopped

METHOD

1 In a large frying pan, heat the oil and fry the sliced onion for 5 mins, until golden and crispy. Add the garlic, ginger and 1 of the chillies, and cook for 1 min.

2 Meanwhile, heat the 2tsp of oil in another frying pan, crack in the eggs and fry until cooked through, but runny.

3 Mix the cooked rice, soy sauce and fish sauce into the onion mixture and stir-fry for 1 min. Add in the pak choi and cook for another 1 min. Stir in the spring onions and the coriander (reserving a little for garnish).

4 Divide the rice between 2 plates, and top each with a fried egg, a sprinkle of sliced red chilli and some more chopped coriander.

PER SERVING: CALS 395 | FAT 18g | SAT FAT 3.5g | CARBS 41g

SPICY TURKISH EGGS WITH TAHINI YOGURT

SPICY TURKISH EGGS WITH TAHINI YOGURT

This shakshuka makes a great breakfast, but can be enjoyed for lunch or dinner too

SERVES 4 • READY IN 25 MINS

INGREDIENTS

3 tbsp olive oil

2 large onions, thinly sliced

1 red, 1 green and 1 yellow pepper, each cut into round slices

3 garlic cloves, finely chopped

½ tsp each cumin seeds, caraway seeds and cayenne pepper

1 tbsp tomato purée

400g | 14oz can chopped tomatoes

A few cherry tomatoes, pierced

1 bunch flat-leaf parsley, chopped

80g | 2.8oz spinach, wilted

1 tsp harissa (optional)

4 eggs

80g | 2.8oz feta, crumbled

2 spring onions, chopped

250g | 8.8oz thick natural yogurt

4 heaped tsp tahini

Pitta breads and olives, to serve

METHOD

1 Heat the oil in a large frying pan. Add the onions, peppers and some seasoning and cook for 3 mins. Add the garlic and cook for a further 1 min.

2 Stir in the spices, tomato purée and all the tomatoes. Simmer uncovered for 10 mins until slightly reduced, then turn off the heat and stir in the parsley, spinach and harissa, if using.

3 Make four small wells in the sauce around the peppers and break an egg into each. Return to the heat and cook over a medium heat for a few mins, until the whites are just set and the yolks still runny. Crumble over the feta and spring onions.

4 Mix together the yogurt and tahini and serve alongside the Turkish eggs, with pitta and olives, if liked.

PER SERVING: CALS 406 | FAT 27g | SAT FAT 8g | CARBS 16g

FOOD FOR THOUGHT
Eggs are packed with choline, a nutrient that boosts concentration and memory.

MEAT, POULTRY & VEG

EDAMAME, COTTAGE CHEESE & NEW POTATO FRITTATA

MEAT, POULTRY & VEG

EDAMAME, COTTAGE CHEESE & NEW POTATO FRITTATA

Edamame beans are immature soybeans and contain many beneficial plant compounds, such as isoflavones and choline

SERVES 4 • READY IN 1 HOUR

INGREDIENTS

300g | 10.6oz new potatoes
100g | 3.5oz frozen edamame beans
5 large eggs
150g | 5.3oz low-fat cottage cheese
2 tsp fresh chopped chives
Pinch of freshly grated nutmeg
30g | 1oz pea shoots, to serve

METHOD

1 Heat the oven to 180°C (160°C fan) | 355°F | gas 4. Cook the potatoes in salted, boiling water for 12-15 mins, until just tender. Drain well and place aside until cool enough to slice.

2 Meanwhile, cook the edamame beans in boiling water for 4-5 mins, until just tender. Drain well. Beat the eggs in a bowl, then stir in the cottage cheese, chopped chives, the nutmeg and some freshly ground black pepper.

3 Lightly grease a medium-sized ovenproof dish and arrange the potato slices and beans in the base. Pour over the egg mixture and bake in the oven for about 30 mins, or until the frittata is golden and set. Cool slightly, then serve in slices, garnished with pea shoots.

PER SERVING: CALS 226 | FAT 10g | SAT FAT 2.3g | CARBS 15g

FOOD FOR THOUGHT

As it contains tryptophan, cottage cheese is a good mood booster. It can also help with relaxation and sleep.

SUPER-GREENS VEG & TOFU STIR-FRY

CHEF'S TIP
You can swap the tofu for prawns, chicken or steak, or cook some extra omelette.

MEAT, POULTRY & VEG

SUPER-GREENS VEG & TOFU STIR-FRY

Tofu is a great plant-based source of protein. It's rich in zinc, which is important for brain health and helps our bodies process fat, carbs and protein

SERVES 4 • READY IN 35 MINS

INGREDIENTS

5 tbsp vegetable oil

2 medium free-range eggs, beaten

Bunch spring onions, finely sliced, plus extra to garnish

4 tbsp plain flour

½ tsp five spice

280g | 10oz block firm tofu, cut into bite-size cubes; patted dry to remove moisture

1 tbsp sesame oil

100g | 3.5oz trimmed green beans, cut into thirds

200g | 7oz baby leaf greens, washed, thick stems discarded and leaves sliced

2 pak choi, cut in quarters or halves, depending on size

FOR THE DRESSING

2 garlic cloves, finely grated

1 tsp ginger, peeled and grated

3 tbsp sesame oil

2 tsp low sodium soy sauce

1 tsp chilli oil

Juice ½ lime, plus wedges to serve

METHOD

1 Heat 1 tbsp vegetable oil in a large, non-stick frying pan or wok. In a bowl, combine the beaten egg with 2 tbsp water and half the spring onions. Pour into the frying pan and tilt to the edges. Cook for a couple of mins until set aside. Set aside to cool, then roll up and slice into thin strips.

2 Mix the flour and five spice with seasoning and toss the tofu in it until evenly coated.

3 Heat the remaining vegetable oil and sesame oil in the pan or wok, then fry the tofu for a few mins on each side until golden and crispy. Remove using a slotted spoon, and set aside on kitchen paper to drain.

4 Add the green beans and greens to the pan and cook for 5 mins, stirring regularly until lightly charred and starting to soften. Add the pak choi and cook for a further 5 mins.

5 Whisk together the dressing ingredients and add half to the wok with the tofu and egg; toss together. Transfer to plates and spoon over the remaining dressing. Garnish with extra spring onion and lime wedges.

PER SERVING: CALS 338 | FAT 43g | SAT FAT 7g | CARBS 15g

RECIPE: JESSICA RANSOM. PHOTO: SEAN CALITZ.

TOFU SKEWERS & NOODLE SALAD

A tasty combo of beautifully marinated tofu with a crunchy, Asian-inspired salad

SERVES 4 • READY IN 35 MINS

INGREDIENTS

- 160g | 5.6oz pack extra firm tofu
- 4 tbsp sweet chilli sauce
- 1 tsp lemongrass paste
- 1 lime, juice and zest
- 150g | 5.3oz cooked rice vermicelli noodles
- 1½ large carrots, shredded
- ½ cucumber, deseeded and shredded
- ½ bunch spring onions, shredded
- 1 tbsp fresh basil, shredded
- 1 tbsp soy sauce
- ½ tbsp toasted sesame oil
- 50g | 1.7oz roasted salted cashew nuts, crushed

METHOD

1 Soak 8 wooden skewers in water for 20 mins. Cut the tofu into cubes and mix together the tofu pieces, 3 tbsp chilli sauce, lemongrass paste, lime juice and zest, then thread on to skewers and set aside.

2 In a large bowl, mix the noodles, carrots, cucumber, spring onions and basil. In a separate bowl, mix the remaining chilli sauce, the soy sauce, sesame oil and 2 tbsp water, drizzle over the noodles and stir.

3 Cook the skewers on a medium high heat for 2 mins on each side in a frying pan or griddle pan. Serve with noodles and top with cashews.

PER SERVING: CALS 166 | FAT 5G | SAT FAT 1G | CARBS 22G

FOOD FOR THOUGHT

A 2020 study by the British Medical Journal, found that participants who consumed more plant-based protein in their diets were 6% less likely to die prematurely than those who ate less protein overall.

MEAT, POULTRY & VEG

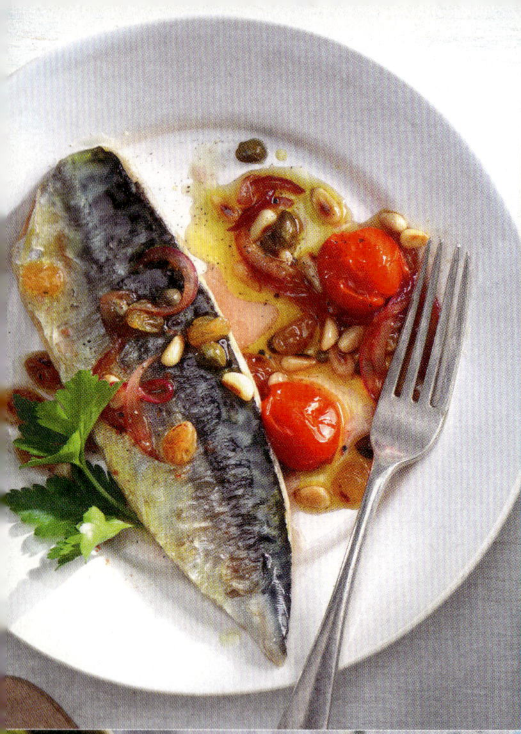
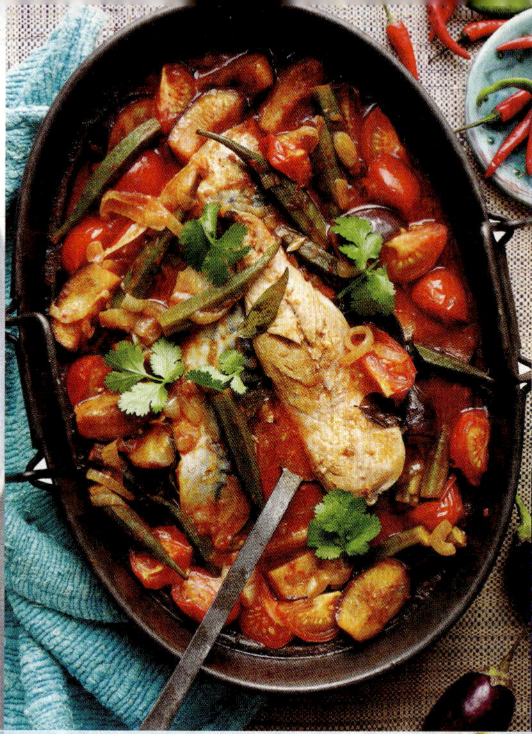
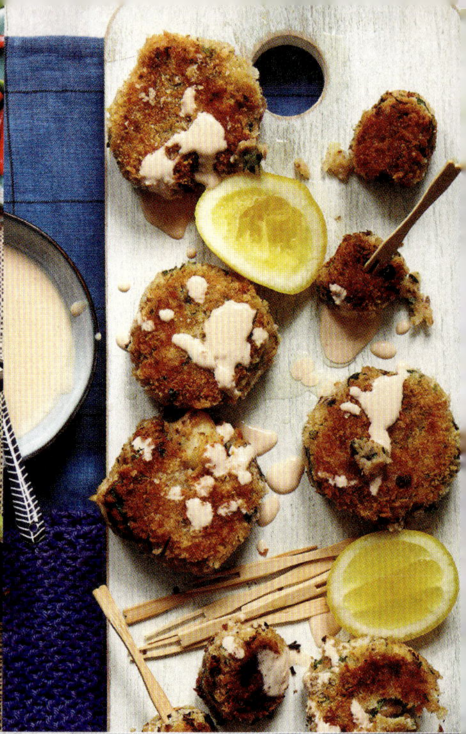
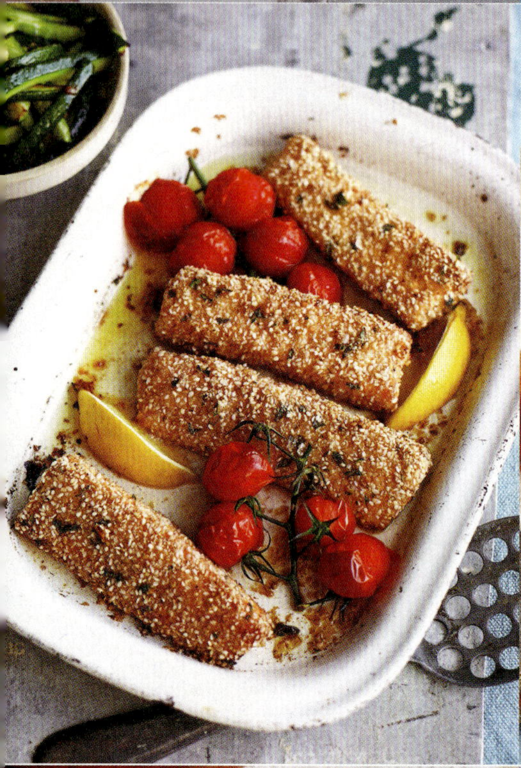
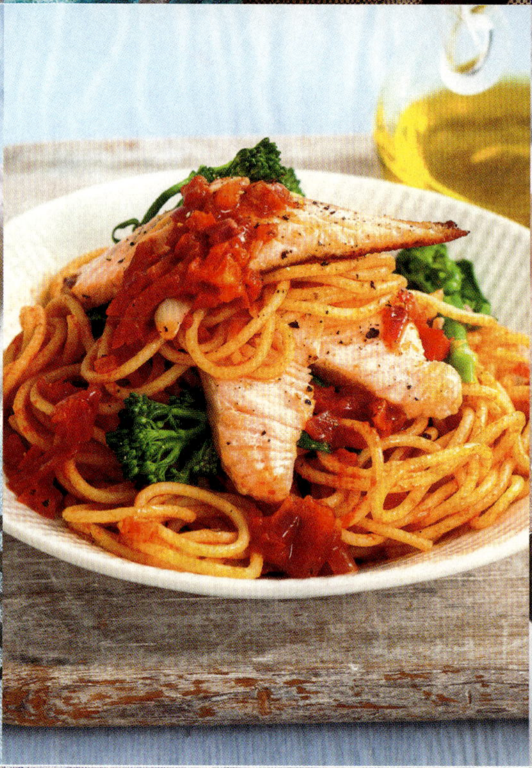
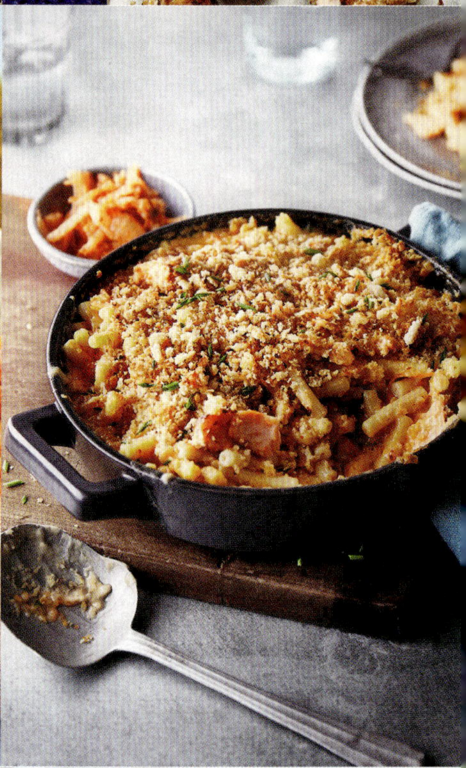
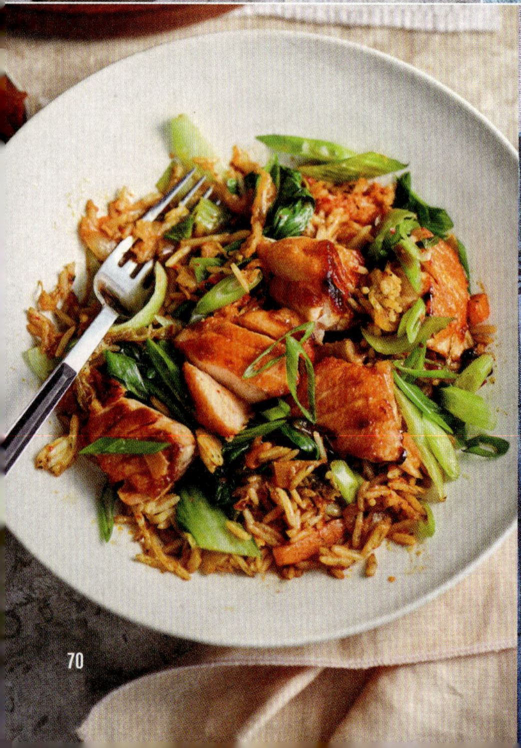
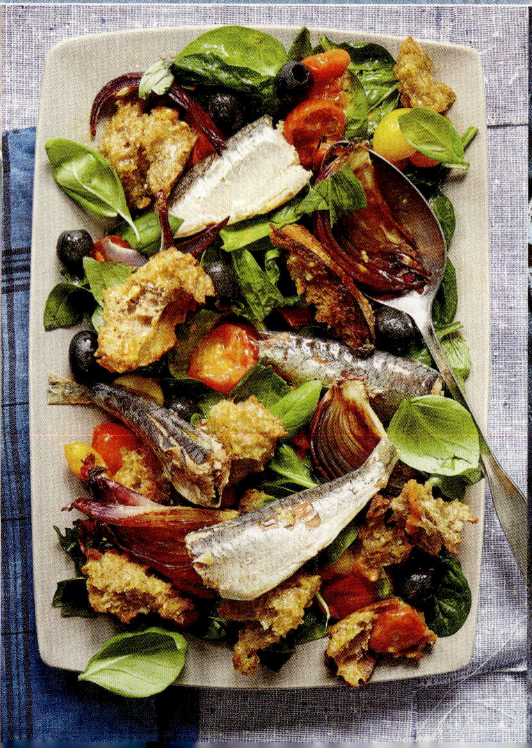
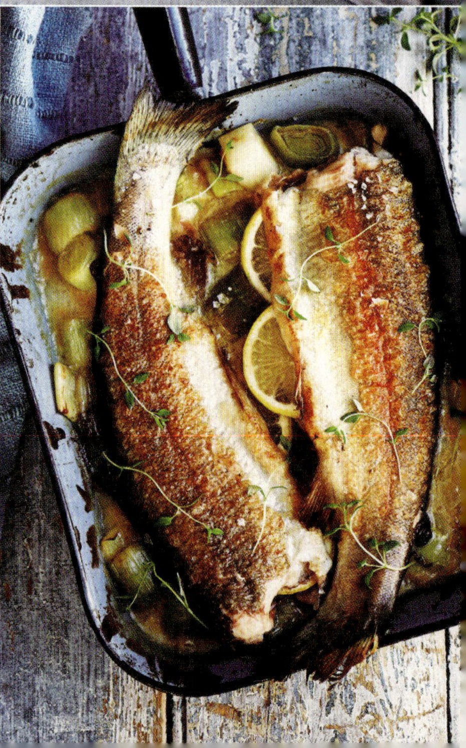

FISH & SEAFOOD

SICILIAN-STYLE MACKEREL 072

MALAYSIAN FISH CURRY 074

FISHCAKES WITH SPICY DRESSING 076

OAT-AND-SESAME-CRUSTED SALMON WITH BLISTERED TOMATOES 078

SALMON & SPAGHETTI BOLOGNESE 080

SALMON MAC 'N' CHEESE WITH KIMCHI 082

MISO-GLAZED SALMON & KIMCHI FRIED RICE 084

SARDINE & SPINACH PANZANELLA 086

ROAST TROUT STUFFED WITH HERB QUINOA & PEPPERS 088

MUSTARD & LEEK TROUT 090

SICILIAN-STYLE MACKEREL

A delicious recipe of light and fresh-tasting fresh mackerel

SERVES 4 • READY IN 25 MINS

INGREDIENTS

- 5 tbsp extra virgin olive oil
- 4 large or 8 small, very fresh mackerel fillets
- 1 small red onion, halved and finely sliced
- 200g | 7oz cherry tomatoes
- 1 garlic clove, sliced
- 3 tbsp red wine vinegar
- 2½ tbsp caster sugar
- 1 heaped tbsp capers, rinsed and drained
- 2 tbsp golden raisins or sultanas
- 2 tbsp pine nuts, toasted handful of flat-leaf parsley leaves
- Crusty bread, to serve

METHOD

1 Put 2 tbsp of the olive oil in a large frying pan set over a medium-high heat. Add the mackerel fillets, skin-side down, and sear for 2 mins, until the skin is golden and crisp.

2 Carefully turn over the fish, cook for 1-2 mins, depending on size, then remove to a plate and set aside. Turn the heat down a little, add the onion and cook, stirring often, for 5 mins.

3 Stir in the tomatoes and garlic, and cook for a further 2 mins. Add the red wine vinegar, sugar, capers, raisins and pine nuts and simmer for 1 min or so. Season to taste, then return the fish to the pan.

4 Warm through, then drizzle with the remaining olive oil and scatter the parsley over. Serve with the crusty bread.

PER SERVING: CALS 613 | FAT 46g | SAT FAT 8g | CARBS 19g

FISH & SEAFOOD

FOOD FOR THOUGHT

This recipe combines oily fish and olive oil, which studies suggest can help keep your mind sharp.

MALAYSIAN FISH CURRY

FISH & SEAFOOD

MALAYSIAN FISH CURRY

Many spices – like those found in curry pastes – have been found to have health benefits

SERVES 4 • READY IN 1 HR 20 MINS

INGREDIENTS

600g | 21.2oz prepared mackerel fillets (about 8)
2 tbsp vegetable oil
1 large onion, peeled, halved and thinly sliced
2-3 tbsp Malaysian Rendang curry paste
24 curry leaves (optional)
4 small aubergines, quartered or 1 medium aubergine, cut into chunks
400ml | 13.5floz can reduced-fat coconut milk
2 tsp tamarind paste
2 tbsp tomato purée
1-2 red and 1-2 green bird's eye (hot) chillies, deseeded, kept whole (optional)
175g | 6.2oz okra, topped and tailed
4 medium-sized tomatoes, each cut into quarters
Coriander leaves, to garnish

METHOD

1 Sprinkle the fish fillets with a little salt and leave for about 20 mins. Meanwhile heat the oil in a large pan, add the onion, sprinkle with salt and fry until it begins to brown.

2 Lower the heat, add the curry paste and curry leaves, if using, and fry gently for 2-3 mins, stirring. Add the aubergine, coconut milk, tamarind paste, purée, chillies, if using, okra and 200ml | 6.8floz water. Simmer for 15 mins. Heat the oven to 200°C (180°C fan) | 390°F | gas 6.

3 Arrange the mackerel snugly, side by side in a roasting tin. Pour over the curry sauce. Tuck the tomato wedges in. Cover with foil and bake for 20-25 mins. Garnish with coriander. Serve with rice.

PER SERVING: CALS 630 | FAT 48g | SAT FAT 17g | CARBS 38.5g

CHEF'S TIP
This curry also works well with other firm-fleshed fish like swordfish, sea bass or halibut for example.

PHOTO: FUTURECONTENTHUB.COM

FISHCAKES WITH SPICY DRESSING

Canned fish is on par with fresh when it comes to getting your omega-3s. These store-cupboard friendly fish cakes make an excellent midweek supper

SERVES 4 • READY IN 55 MINS

INGREDIENTS

- 450g | 1lb potatoes, peeled and halved
- 400g | 14oz tin pilchards in tomato sauce
- Zest and juice of 1 lemon, plus extra wedges to serve
- Half a bunch parsley, chopped
- 1 bunch chives, finely chopped
- 1 small onion, finely chopped
- 1 egg, beaten
- 60g | 2oz panko breadcrumbs

FOR THE DIPPING SAUCE

- 3 tbsp crème fraîche
- 3 tbsp mayonnaise
- 3 tbsp tomato sauce from the pilchard tin
- 1-2 tsp Tabasco, or pinch cayenne pepper

METHOD

1 Steam the potatoes for 20 mins or until tender. Roughly mash with a fork while still warm.

2 Drain the pilchards, reserving 3tbsp of the tomato sauce for the dipping sauce, then mix the fish into the mashed potato with the zest and juice, herbs and onion, and stir until well until combined. Form into 4 large fishcakes, then dip in beaten egg, then in breadcrumbs, to coat.

3 Heat oil in a frying pan and fry the fishcakes for 3-4 mins on either side, until nicely golden and cooked through.

4 To make the sauce, combine all ingredients in a small bowl. Serve with the hot fishcakes, lemon wedges and a big salad on the side.

PER SERVING: CALS 425 | FAT 21.5G | SAT FAT 5.5G | CARBS 24G

CHEF'S TIP
You can swap the pilchards for any oily fish you have.

FISH & SEAFOOD

OAT-&-SESAME-CRUSTED SALMON WITH BLISTERED TOMATOES

FOOD FOR THOUGHT

Flaxseed, nuts, seeds and seaweed are excellent sources of omega-3 for vegetarians and vegans.

FISH & SEAFOOD

OAT-&-SESAME-CRUSTED SALMON WITH BLISTERED TOMATOES

Tomatoes and other bright red veg contain lycopene, a powerful antioxidant that's linked to long-term memory and cognitive health

SERVES 4 • READY IN 30 MINS

INGREDIENTS

- 4 tbsp oatmeal
- 1 tsp oregano, chopped, or ¼ tsp dried oregano
- 4 tbsp sesame seeds
- 1½ lemons
- 4 skinless salmon fillets (about 140g | 5oz each)
- 2 tbsp olive oil
- 2 courgettes, trimmed and cut into sticks
- 1 garlic clove, crushed
- 200g | 7oz cherry tomatoes on the vine

METHOD

1 Heat the oven to 180°C (160°C fan) | 355°F | gas 4. Combine the oatmeal, oregano and sesame seeds in a shallow dish. Squeeze the juice of 1 lemon into another shallow dish.

2 Dip the fish in the lemon juice then the oatmeal mixture, turning to coat, then arrange on a lined baking tray and drizzle with 1 tbsp of the olive oil. Bake for 15 mins, until golden.

3 Toss the courgettes with the garlic and the remaining oil. Season well and spread over another baking tray. Roast for 15 mins.

4 Cut the remaining half lemon into wedges and add to the fish tray, along with the tomatoes. Turn the courgettes and return both trays to the oven for another 10 mins.

PER SERVING: CALS 500 | FAT 35g | SAT FAT 6g | CARBS 13g

SALMON & SPAGHETTI BOLOGNESE

SALMON & SPAGHETTI BOLOGNESE

Swap the meat and make salmon the star of this new family favourite with a twist

SERVES 4 • READY IN 35 MINS

INGREDIENTS

- 250g | 8.8oz salmon fillet, sliced
- Finely grated zest and juice of 1 lemon
- 2 tbsp olive oil
- 1 vegetable stock cube or jellied 'stock pot' (ie Knorr)
- 250g | 8.8oz spaghetti
- 150g | 5.3oz Tenderstem broccoli
- 1 onion, chopped
- 2 garlic cloves, crushed
- 1 red pepper, deseeded and chopped
- 200g | 7oz passata

METHOD

1 Heat the oven to 200°C (180°C fan) | 390°F | gas 6. Put the salmon on a non-stick baking tray. Season generously with salt and freshly ground black pepper and sprinkle over lemon zest and juice, and 1 tsp olive oil. Bake for 10 mins.

2 Meanwhile, add the Stock Pot to a pan of water, bring to the boil, add the spaghetti and cook for 10 mins. Add the broccoli for the final 3 mins of cooking time.

3 Heat the remaining oil in a frying pan, add the onion, garlic and pepper, and simmer gently for 5 mins. Add the passata and simmer for a few mins.

4 Drain the pasta and broccoli, and combine with the sauce. Serve with the salmon.

PER SERVING: CALS 445 | FAT 14g | SAT FAT 2.5g | CARBS 6g

FOOD FOR THOUGHT

Incorporating oily fish into traditionally meat dishes like this is a great way to get more omega-3 while also reducing your meat intake.

FISH & SEAFOOD

SALMON MAC 'N' CHEESE WITH KIMCHI

FISH & SEAFOOD

SALMON MAC 'N' CHEESE WITH KIMCHI

Kimchi adds a punch to this creamy, cheesy pasta with smoky salmon – you could swap it for sauerkraut or add cornichons

SERVES 6 • READY IN 40 MINS

INGREDIENTS

- 250g | 8.8oz macaroni
- 50g | 1.8oz butter
- 3 tbsp plain flour
- 500ml | 17floz | 2⅛ cups whole milk, warmed
- 300g | 10.5oz cheese (mix Cheddar, Gruyère or whatever needs using up), grated
- A few pinches freshly grated nutmeg
- 200g | 7oz kimchi
- 2 hot smoked salmon fillets, flaked
- 3 tbsp panko breadcrumbs
- Chives, chopped (optional)

METHOD

1 Heat the oven to 220°C (200°C fan) | 430°F | gas 7. Boil the macaroni in a pan of salted water for 2 mins less than the pack instructions; drain and set aside.

2 Melt the butter in a large pan, then stir in the flour and season. Cook for a few minutes, then slowly whisk in the warmed milk until smooth and cook, stirring, until thickened. Stir in most of the cheese until melted and season with nutmeg.

3 Add the drained pasta to the cheese sauce with the kimchi and salmon. Mix to combine, then decant into an ovenproof dish. Scatter with the remaining cheese and the breadcrumbs. Bake for 15-20 mins, until golden and bubbling. Serve with herbs and more kimchi.

PER SERVING: CALS 616 | FAT 30g | SAT FAT 18g | CARBS 54g

CHEF'S TIP
This is a great option for making ahead. Cover the dish and chill for up to 1-2 days. Reheat until piping hot, adding an extra 10 mins or so to the cooking time.

MISO-GLAZED SALMON & KIMCHI FRIED RICE

MISO-GLAZED SALMON & KIMCHI FRIED RICE

Flavour-packed condiments do the heavy lifting in this speedy dinner

SERVES 2 • READY IN 15 MINS

INGREDIENTS

- 2 tbsp olive oil
- 2 sustainably sourced skinless salmon fillets, each cut into 3 pieces
- 3 tbsp miso sauce (such as Miso Tasty Sweet & Savoury)
- 200g | 7oz kimchi, drained and roughly chopped, plus 2 tbsp drained liquid
- 200g | 7oz pack stir-fry vegetables, roughly chopped
- 250g | 8.8oz cooked rice

TO SERVE

- Finely chopped spring onions
- Soy sauce
- Extra kimchi

METHOD

1 Heat 1 tbsp oil in a wok, or a large pan, over a high heat. Cook the salmon for 3-4 mins, turning regularly until golden on all sides and just cooked through. Brush with half the miso sauce and set aside.

2 Return the wok, or pan, to the heat with another 1 tbsp oil. Add the drained kimchi and cook over high heat for 3-4 mins until a little charred. Add the greens and cook for 1 min to soften, then add the rice, the remaining miso sauce and 2 tbsp kimchi liquid. Cook for another 3-4 mins until the rice is piping hot.

3 Toss the salmon back through the fried rice and serve. Add finely sliced spring onions, a dash of soy and extra kimchi, if you like.

PER SERVING: CALS 726 | FAT 37g | SAT FAT 7g | CARBS 54g

FOOD FOR THOUGHT

The combination of omega-3-rich salmon, fermented miso and kimchi gives this dish a variety of brain-boosting nutrients.

FISH & SEAFOOD

SARDINE & SPINACH PANZANELLA

FISH & SEAFOOD

SARDINE & SPINACH PANZANELLA

A hearty summer salad that is packed with flavour and nutrition

SERVES 4 • READY IN 35 MINS

INGREDIENTS

1 red onion, cut into wedges
2 tbsp olive oil
250g | 8.8oz tomatoes, halved
150g | 5.3oz wholemeal bread, roughly torn into chunks
1 garlic clove, crushed
Thin strips of rind from ½ lemon
2x 120g | 4.2oz cans sardines
75g | 2.6oz spinach leaves
45g | 1.5oz black olives
30g | 1oz basil leaves, torn

FOR THE DRESSING

1 garlic clove, crushed
125ml | 4.2floz | ½ cup extra-virgin olive oil
3 tbsp white wine vinegar
1 tsp Dijon mustard

METHOD

1 Heat the oven to 180°C (160°C fan) | 355°F | gas 4. Place the onion wedges on a baking tray, drizzle with 1 tbsp olive oil and roast for 15 mins. Add the tomatoes and roast for a further 10 mins.

2 Put the bread on a separate baking tray, drizzle with 1 tbsp oil, scatter over the garlic and lemon rind and roast for 10 mins.

3 Combine all the dressing ingredients, stir in the roasted tomatoes and season to taste. Mix together the onion, bread, sardines, spinach, olives and basil on a platter and pour over the tomato dressing to serve.

PER SERVING: CALS 532 | FAT 41G | SAT FAT 5G | CARBS 19G

FOOD FOR THOUGHT

Sardines are a nutritional bargain – rich in fatty acids, protein and calcium.

ROAST TROUT STUFFED WITH HERB QUINOA & PEPPERS

This showstopping supper is elegant enough for entertaining. If you want to use salmon instead it might need longer to cook

SERVES 6 • READY IN 1 HR 5 MINS

INGREDIENTS

- 4 red, yellow or orange peppers
- 2 tbsp olive oil, plus extra for drizzling
- 125g | 4.4oz quinoa
- 300ml | 10.5floz | 1¼ cups vegetable stock
- 100g | 3.5oz stoned olives, roughly chopped
- 2 large handfuls of soft herbs, such as parsley, mint, basil, chives, coriander and a little tarragon, chopped
- Grated zest of 1 lemon and a little juice
- 3 tbsp pine nuts, toasted
- 2x 500g | 17oz sides trout or salmon, cleaned and pin-boned

METHOD

1 Heat the oven to 230°C (210°C fan) | 445°F | gas 8. For the stuffing, slice the 'cheeks' from the peppers, leaving the seeds and pith behind, and arrange on an oiled baking tray, skin-side up. Drizzle with oil and roast for about 20 mins, until nicely charred. Put in a covered bowl and once cool, peel off the skins.

2 Turn down the oven to 170°C (150°C fan) | 340°F | gas 3. Rinse the quinoa in a sieve and put it in a pan with the stock. Bring to the boil and simmer for 16-18 mins then set aside. Once cool, stir in 2 tbsp olive oil and the remaining ingredients (except the fish).

3 Lay out 5 x 30cm | 12" lengths of kitchen string across an oiled baking tray, 4cm | 1½" apart. Put one fish side, skin-side down, on top, ensuring the string is evenly spaced. Season the fish and spoon the stuffing on top, pressing it down firmly. Season the second fish side, then lay it on top, skin-side up. Tie up with the string. The fish can be prepared to this stage in advance and kept in the fridge for later.

4 Bring to room temperature before cooking. Bake for 15-20 mins until it just flakes when pressed. Serve with greens.

PER SERVING: CALS 418 | FAT 32g | SAT FAT 2g | CARBS 15g

FISH & SEAFOOD

CHEF'S TIP
The fish can be prepared to the end of step 2 in advance and kept in the fridge until it's time to bake.

MUSTARD & LEEK TROUT

FISH & SEAFOOD

MUSTARD & LEEK TROUT

Mustard not only packs a flavour punch, it is also rich in brain-boosting glucosinolates

SERVES 2 • READY IN 1 HR

INGREDIENTS

- 1 tbsp olive oil
- 2 prepared rainbow trout, heads removed if you prefer
- 3 leeks, trimmed and sliced
- 2 banana shallots, finely chopped
- 2 garlic cloves, crushed
- 1 tbsp plain flour
- 150ml | 5floz | ⅔ cup fish or vegetable stock
- 2 lemons – reserve 4 slices and take the juice from the remainder
- 2 tsp Dijon mustard
- ½ tsp coarse ground black pepper
- Few sprigs of thyme
- 1 tbsp chopped flat parsley

METHOD

1 Heat the oven to 200°C (180°C fan) | 390°F | gas 6. Heat the oil in an ovenproof frying pan or casserole dish big enough to hold both fish. Brown the trout until golden, then set aside.

2 Turn down the heat and sweat the leek, shallots and garlic for 10 mins. Whisk the flour into the stock until smooth; add to the pan along with the lemon juice, mustard and black pepper, let it bubble for a few mins.

3 Stuff the fish with the lemon slices and a little of the thyme. Set both fish in the pan, sprinkle over the rest of the herbs, cover and bake for 20 mins.

PER SERVING: CALS 790 | FAT 29g | SAT FAT 6g | CARBS 8.5g

FOOD FOR THOUGHT

Public Health England recommends that we should eat at least two portions of fish each week, with one being oily.

92

SWEETS & DRINKS

KEFIR FRUIT & BRAN BOWL 094

BEST BLUEBERRY CRUMBLE MUFFINS 096

NUT, SEED & BERRY CRUMBLE 098

APPLE & BLUEBERRY FLAPJACKS 100

SUPER BERRY BREAKFAST BOWL 102

CRANBERRY MUESLI BARS 104

DARK CHOCOLATE MOUSSE 106

SUGAR PLUMS 108

SUPER SMOOTHIES 110

KEFIR FRUIT & BRAN BOWL

SWEETS & DRINKS

KEFIR FRUIT & BRAN BOWL

This fresh and fruity snack is packed with vitamins, fibre and probiotics

SERVES 1 • READY IN 5 MINS

INGREDIENTS

60g | 2oz hulled strawberries, sliced

30g | 1oz peeled kiwi, sliced

85g | 3oz kefir (1.5% fat, such as Lowicz Kefir Yoghurt Drink)

20g | 0.7oz pomegranate seeds

5g | 0.2oz All-Bran, or any similar high-bran cereal

METHOD

1 Arrange the prepared strawberries and sliced kiwi in the base of a small serving dish.

2 Spoon over the kefir, covering the fruit, and then scatter with the pomegranate seeds and All-Bran. Serve immediately.

PER SERVING: CALS 265 | FAT 2.5g | SAT FAT 0.6g | CARBS 31.5g

FOOD FOR THOUGHT

A 2023 study found that Lactobacillus – a probiotic bacteria found in kefir – can help the body manage stress and may even reduce the risk of depression.

PHOTO: FUTURECONTENTHUB.COM

BEST BLUEBERRY CRUMBLE MUFFINS

With juicy blueberries and a tasty crumble topping, you can't beat a muffin with a coffee

MAKES 12 • READY IN 45-50 MINS

INGREDIENTS

- 300g | 10.5oz plain flour
- 150g | 5.3oz caster sugar
- 1 tbsp baking powder
- 225g | 8oz blueberries
- 2 free-range medium eggs
- 150ml | 5floz | ⅔ cup whole milk
- 150g | 5.3oz unsalted butter, melted

FOR THE CRUMBLE TOPPING

- 45g | 1.5oz unsalted butter, cold, cubed
- 75g | 2.6oz plain flour
- 2 tsp cinnamon
- 2 tbsp demerara sugar
- 1 tbsp pumpkin seeds
- 10 pecans halves, roughly chopped or broken

YOU WILL NEED

12-hole deep muffin tin lined with paper cases

METHOD

1 Heat the oven to 200°C (180°C fan) | 390°F | gas 6. For the crumble topping, using your fingertips, rub the butter into the flour. Once the mixture starts to clump, stir in the cinnamon, sugar, pumpkin seeds and pecans. Chill.

2 For the muffins, put the flour, sugar and baking powder into a large bowl with a pinch of salt. Toss through the blueberries.

3 Beat together the eggs, milk and melted butter. Make a well in the flour mix, then pour in the egg mixture. Stir briefly, until smooth and combined.

4 Divide evenly between the muffin cases and top with the crumble. Bake for 25-30 mins or until well risen and golden.

PER MUFFIN: CALS 354 | FAT 16g | SAT FAT 8g | CARBS 46g

CHEF'S TIP
This recipe works well with frozen blueberries or other fruits.

SWEETS & DRINKS

NUT, SEED AND BERRY CRUMBLE

SWEETS & DRINKS

NUT, SEED & BERRY CRUMBLE

Add texture and flavour to an old favourite, with the addition of nutritious nuts and seeds

SERVES 6 • READY IN 55 MINS

INGREDIENTS

6 apples, peeled and cut into chunks
4 tbsp maple syrup
250g | 8.8oz blueberries

FOR THE TOPPING

80g | 2.8oz butter
100g | 3.5oz quinoa flakes
50g | 1.8oz oats
4 tbsp light brown sugar
50g | 1.8oz nuts
1 tsp ground cinnamon
2 tbsp each sesame, sunflower and pumpkin seeds
Half-fat crème fraîche, to serve

METHOD

1 Heat the oven to 200°C (180°C fan) | 390°F | gas 6. Toss the apples in the maple syrup on a baking tray and bake for 15 mins.

2 Meanwhile, make the topping. Rub the butter into the quinoa flakes and oats until it resembles coarse breadcrumbs. Stir in the sugar, nuts, cinnamon and seeds.

3 Put the apples in an ovenproof dish and stir in the blueberries, then top with the crumble topping. Return to the oven and bake for 25 mins.

4 Once the crumble is golden and bubbling, remove and serve with crème fraîche.

PER SERVING: CALS 393 | FAT 21g | SAT FAT 8.5g | CARBS 41g

FOOD FOR THOUGHT

Research suggests that eating a handful of blueberries a day can improve memory and cognition.

PHOTO: FUTURECONTENTHUB.COM

/ APPLE & BLUEBERRY FLAPJACKS

APPLE & BLUEBERRY FLAPJACKS

These delicious treats will help lift you out of an afternoon slump

MAKES 16 • READY IN 40 MINS + COOLING TIME

INGREDIENTS

200g | 7oz unsalted butter
200g | 7oz caster sugar
150g | 5.3oz runny honey
425g | 15oz porridge oats
2 red apples, peeled and grated
¾ tsp ground cinnamon
100g | 3.5oz dried blueberries
75g | 2.6oz sunflower seeds
75g | 2.6oz Brazil nuts, chopped

YOU WILL NEED

A 20x30cm | 8x12" baking tray, greased, base lined with baking paper

METHOD

1 Heat oven to 180°C (160°C fan) | 355°F | gas 4. Melt the butter, sugar and honey in a medium-sized saucepan until dissolved, then mix until well combined. Remove from heat and stir in remaining ingredients, mixing well to coat evenly.

2 Spoon into the prepared tray and spread and flatten to create a smooth top. Bake for 35 mins, until golden.

3 Leave in the tray to cool, but score the flapjacks into 16 squares while still warm. Once completely cool, cut into squares. The flapjacks will keep in an airtight container for 2-3 days.

PER FLAPJACK: CALS 360 | FAT 18G | SAT FAT 7.5G | CARBS 45G

FOOD FOR THOUGHT

Slow-energy-releasing oats are a good way to keep your blood sugar levels, energy and mood stable.